Policing a Society in Turmoil

By the same author

- — Crisis in Law Enforcement
- — Human Rights and Law Enforcement
- — Law Enforcement and Cross Border Terrorism
- — Reflections and Reminiscences of Police Officers
- — Riding Memory's Chariot
- — Terrorism Around the World: Challenges and Responses
- — Trafficking in Women and Children: Myths and Realities
- — Violent Neighbourhood Turbulence in Pakistan and Afghanistan

---

About the Author

Sankar Sen is a distinguished member of the Indian Police Service. He was the Director of National Police Academy, Hyderabad and Director General of the National Human Rights Commission. He was awarded Police Medal for Meritorious Services and President's Medal for Distinguished Service. He has authored a number of books and his articles appear in well-known newspapers, magazines and journals in and outside the country. Presently, he is a Senior Fellow at the Institute of Social Sciences, New Delhi.

Policing a Society in Turmoil

Sankar Sen

CONCEPT PUBLISHING COMPANY PVT. LTD.
NEW DELHI-110059

ISBN-13: 978-93-86682-01-7

First Published 2017

Published and Printed by

Concept Publishing Company Pvt. Ltd.
Regd. Office:
A/15-16, Commercial Block, Mohan Garden,
New Delhi-110059 (INDIA)
Phones : 25351460, 25351794, *Fax* : 091-11-25357109
E-mail : publishing@conceptpub.com,
Website: www.conceptpub.com

Cataloging in Publication Data—DK Courtesy: D.K. Agencies (P) Ltd. <docinfo@dkagencies.com>

Sen, Sankar, 1936- author.
Policing a society in turmoil / Sankar Sen.
pages cm
Includes index.
ISBN 9789386682017

1. Police—India. 2. Police. 3. Social problems—India. 4. Social problems. 5. Criminal justice, Administration of—India. 6. Criminal justice, Administration of. I. Title.

HV8247.S46 2017 DDC 363.20954 23

Preface

Policing a democratic society is a challenging job and this is more so when it is beset with problems of rising crime, lawlessness, violent terrorism and poor governance. Indian police today is grappling with myriads of problems which are increasingly becoming more complex and intractable. Events in the violent neighbourhood are also dark and ominous. India has to contend with cross-border terrorism sponsored by its neighbour. Transnational terrorism spearheaded by Taliban and Islamic State (IS) also pose formidable threats. Islamic caliphate in Syria and Iraq is now suffering setbacks and shrinking, but it has sponsored and outsourced terrorism through its followers in different countries of the world. India is very much in its radar. Recent gruesome terrorist violence in Dhaka shows that the terrorists will seek to exploit the vulnerabilities of India and target it for devastating attacks.

The police problems and constraints are many, and police is also seriously handicapped by the malfunctioning of the criminal justice system. Cases are mounting in the courts of law and the wheel of justice moves at a snail's pace. The result is that people seek to take laws in their own hands. Law enforcement authorities opt for shortcut extra-legal methods and show scant respect for human rights. The articles in the book dwell on all these problems of policing a society in turmoil in India and suggest some remedial strategies. It is hoped that the book will be of interest to the law makers, law enforcement officers and informed members of the public.

Contents

Chapter 1

Why the Police do not Change?

Public distrust of police in India remains pronounced and this distrustful negative attitude towards the police has not changed with the passage of time. It has perhaps become more pronounced. During the British colonial rule the police was rightly viewed as the agent and instrument of imperial power. But even after Independence, the image of the police has witnessed no improvement. The Police Commission of 1902 (the First All India Police Commission appointed by Lord Curzon) described Indian police as a "bugbear, a strong arm of the state that harasses and seldom helps the public".

In the sixties when we joined the Indian Police Service, the public perception of the police was poor, if not hostile. Many of my friends and relations cautioned me against joining the service and turning into a sadistic bully. At that time many stories, some of them purely apocryphal, of violence and brutality by the police highlighted in the print media were accepted by the credulous public as true. The image of the police was that of a hated bogey man. The picture has not changed even six decades after Independence. Unfortunately, the police remain alienated from the public and viewed with distrust and hostility.

In his seminal work on Indian police, Dr. David Bayley has said that in India and in other South Asian countries that had been under colonial rule, in contrast to many countries in the West, the public seek to avoid the police and the avoidance-syndrome is more pronounced in North India than in South. There is a saying in Bengali folklore that contact with the police entails more trouble than encountering a tiger, and hence one should remain miles away from the police.

The police are also reconciled to the hard fact that the public will never understand the problems and dilemmas of the police and remain constantly critical. During training in the National Police Academy (where IPS officers are trained) and State Police Training Institutions, the police officers are lectured on the indispensability of police-public cooperation for efficient functioning of the police. Without public cooperation, difficult and hazardous occupation of policing becomes more complex and unsatisfying. But after they leave the portals of the training institutions to face the glare and grime of policing in the field, they are advised by their police seniors to quickly forget and bury five fathoms deep what they have been taught in the training institutes. Police work is tough and very often disagreeable methods have to be adopted to deal with criminals and law breakers. In law enforcement, end justifies the means and shortcut extra-legal methods are inescapable. During my practical training as the Assistant Superintendent of Police in Cuttack district of Odisha, the Superintendent of Police, a competent, no-nonsense, rough-hewn officer, told me in no uncertain terms that abstract and humane principles of policing taught in the classrooms are miles away from the tough realities of the police job. This is the persistent and overwhelming dilemma of policing.

Political masters also expect the police to adopt short cut, and what in police parlance called third degree methods, to contain the depredations of the vicious criminals. They, however, unabashedly turn round to pillory the police if things go awry and there is public outcry against police misdemeanour. Police leaders, who sometimes wink at these dubious methods forget that this is a slippery-slope and once the law enforcers turn into law breakers there would be end of good policing and many innocent people will become victims of police abuse of power. One of the former Chief Justices of Odisha High Court, told me during my training period that in enforcing law and order the police have to constantly remember that order has to be maintained through law. Otherwise, dacoits can maintain better order than the police.

During the British rule, the police loyally subserved the interests of the colonial masters. Though there were many competent officers of integrity, who efficiently maintained law and order and earned people's respect, the police, by and large, were ruthless in dealing with the freedom fighters. They remained rulers' police and not people's police. The police today also follow the same tradition and remain totally beholden to the politicians of the ruling party. This has further alienated it from the public. The old order instead of disappearing after the departure of the erstwhile rulers has continued under the new dispensation. Efforts of insulation of the police from extraneous pressures and influence, despite directives of the apex court, have not worked out because of the unyielding opposition of the political masters, who are dead set against such reforms.

Though the British rulers unabashedly used and misused the police to further their imperial interests, it enacted laws to prevent misuse of police powers against common people. The Indian Evidence Act lays down (Section 25) that the confession before the police is inadmissible in evidence and statements before the police during investigation of cases are not to be signed by the witnesses. (Section 162 of the Criminal Procedure Code). These provisions based on distrust of the police continue in statutes and recommendations by jurists (Report of the Malimath Commission, Report of the 14th Law Commission headed by Setelvad) go unheeded. The general perception of the public is that police attitude and *modus operandi* have not changed and hence trust cannot be reposed in them. The outcome is that the police adopt dubious methods to circumvent the law and earn public opprobrium.

During the British regime, the police were discouraged to develop closer relationship with the public. There was an underlying fear that this will affect strict law enforcement and handicap police in dealing with the native populace. The Police Act of 1861, in specifying police duties, fails to mention the important duty of obtaining public support and cooperation without which the police work becomes onerous and irksome. In Independent India also, the hiatus between the police and the public continues. There is the constant fear of the police leaders and political bosses that closer relationship with the public will erode fear of the police and hamper law enforcement and order maintenance. Community policing experiments in India, by and large, have not been successful because the police have not given the public a meaningful role in planning and supervision of police operations. There is community's justified scepticism that the police are indulging in some kind of public relations gimmick and are not really interested in true community policing.

In the past, the police constables, who constitute 70 per cent of the force were treated as errand boys, not to be given responsible police functions needing application of mind. The Police Commission of 1902 says that responsible police work need not be delegated to them. The position of the constabulary almost remains the same. They have not been empowered and continued as, one perceptive police writer puts it, "spear carriers" in the background of the police drama. Many of them after 30 to 45 years of service, retire unsung and unhonoured in the same rank they joined.

Today, many bright and qualified men and women with high academic accomplishments are joining the police in senior leadership positions. Quite a few of them are from IITs and IIMs, but they have for a variety of causes, some of them systemic, failed to change the structure and soul of the Indian police. Old order continues and not many signs of change are visible.

Chapter 2

Hashimpura Massacre: A Blot on Uttar Pradesh Police

The acquittal of all the accused persons in the 1987 Hashimpura massacre is a shocking miscarriage of justice. In this brutal episode, 42 persons were shot dead in cold blood by the personnel of 41 Battalion of Provincial Armed Constabulary (PAC) of UP. All the victims were Muslims. The incident took place in 1987 and the verdict of acquittal came in 2015. The Delhi Court, which has been hearing the matter since 2006, noted that the accused persons had to be acquitted because the prosecution failed to identify them beyond reasonable doubt as the killers. The evidence adduced by the prosecution was circumstantial and sketchy and was considered by the court as inadequate to convict the accused persons. In this case, as the testimonies of the survivors and other evidence established that during a communal frenzy in Meerut about 50 men of Mohalla Hashimpura were abducted by an Unit of 41st Battalion of PAC in a truck. Five men miraculously survived this cold blooded massacre, and narrated this horrific crime to the trial court.

PAC's history shows that though a disciplined force, it had displayed promounced communal bias on several occasions. The PAC, before its mutiny in 1973, was a disciplined force and excelled in various law and order situations all-over the country, especially in the North-East, where it was extensively used for counter-insurgency operations. But in communal disturbances, it had often betrayed a partisan and anti-Muslim bias, for which, it never commanded the confidence of the minorities. The Idgah incident in Muradabad in 1980 was a shocking exposure of the communal behaviour of the PAC; but no steps had been taken to discipline the force and bring about any structural changes. The shocking culmination was that during disturbances in Meerut in 1987, many young Muslims were picked up by the PAC in Hashimpura and killed in cold blood at two different places in Ghaziabad.

It is ironical to note that during the widespread riots of 1980 in Uttar Pradesh, the then Chief Minister of UP V.P. Singh took the decision to raise some battalions of PAC as mixed battalions with a fair representation of minorities, as Vishesh Seva Dal (VSD). However, proper representation of minorities in these special units was effectively scuttled by vested interests so that the representation of the Muslims remained between 3 or 4 per cent, which was the case with other normal PAC battalions. It is a sad and shocking fact that men involved in kidnapping and killings of Muslim youths in Hashimpura belonged to one of these VSD battalions, which were raised to protect the minorities and treat them fairly.

The investigation and prosecution of the case which dragged on for 28 years revealed the appalling malfunctioning of the Criminal Justice System and a shocking travesty of justice. It took nine years for the police to file charge sheet and even after that the case progressed at a snail's pace in the court of law. The accused persons were determinedly evading appearance in the court of law on various pretexts. Between 1994 and 2000, 23 bailable warrants were issued against the accused persons, who at last surrendered before a Ghaziabad court in 2000. All of them were promptly released on bail and returned to service. The case was transferred to Delhi in 2002, and the trial began in 2006. When the trial began, 3 of the 19 accused persons were dead. Because of the abnormal delay, the witnesses could not recall properly the chain of events and discrepancies crept in their accounts. There were all-out efforts to suborn the witnesses.

Investigation of the case by the state CID was shoddy, if not dubious. Prosecution could not establish how the accused personnel were identified since there were hundreds of personnel on duty. This is baffling. Proper scrutiny of duty charts would have indicated the location of each member of the force on that fateful day. The dubious and complicit nature of investigation is proved by the fact that recovery of the weapons was done poorly. Only 1 bullet and 5 cartridges could be recovered. Proper search of the area was not made to recover the bullets. Because of shoddy investigation, the prosecutors could not prove that a particular truck was used in the commission of the crime. There was clear and palpable complicity of the police investigators and it is very disquieting to note that senior supervisory officers did precious little to ensure that investigation was carried out on proper and scientific lines. There was palpable supervisory cowardice and incompetence.

Vibhuti Narain Rai, then Superintendent of Police, Ghaziabad had given a chilling description of the events on the night of 22-23 May, 1987, and the gory details of the brutal massacre. However, there was also failure on the part of Ghaziabad police to take well-measured steps to preserve the scene of crime and take the vehicle in custody.

The judiciary also has not covered itself with glory. It failed to take energetic steps to speed up the trial. There were repeated adjournments. Serious strictures were not passed against the State Government and the police administration for their dilly-dallying tactics. The material pieces of evidence were either destroyed or allowed to disappear. This was a pre-meditated omission to dilute the prosecution case and shield the accused. Both the police and the prosecution were allowed to get away with such gross dereliction of duty because they enjoyed the blessings of the political masters.

Justice Malimath Committee on reforms on the criminal justice system made the salutary recommendation that the quest for truth should be the lodestar of the criminal justice system. Courts should be empowered to summon any person as a witness it considered necessary and issue directions to the investigating officer whenever necessary to help the court in the search for truth. The court has to play a dynamic and proactive role in the process. The manner in which the judge made no endeavour on his part for search for truth is indeed shocking.

Successive Governments in UP had done nothing to monitor the case and see that justice is done to the victims and perpetrators of the horrendous massacre are brought to book. The Congress, SP and the BSP, which ruled UP during these years, despite proclaiming concern for the safety of the Muslims, did little to ensure vigorous investigation and speedy trial of the case.

The chain of events shows how the case meandered in the court of law. The movement was glacially slow. Last prosecution witnesses were examined on 8th December, 2011, but prosecution evidence closed in 2014 and the judgement was pronounced on 21st March, 2015. The delay only benefited the accused persons. The judicial system, to put it mildly, proved apathetic and sluggish.

The Hashimpura carnage highlights the need for better representation of minorities, and particularly the Muslim, in the police force. In 2012, the Muslim representation in the police throughout the country was 8 per cent. There is no police force, except Jammu & Kashmir, where the Muslims serve in the force in proportion to the general population. There should no discrimination against recruitment of minorities at any level. Reservation of Muslims, in the recruitment may meet Constitutional and legal hurdles. The Sacchar Committee report advocated reservation for minorities. Few in India will like to see another additional layer in State institutions. Great Britain abjures quotas altogether but follows the policy of positive action to help under-represented minorities to compete more effectively in selection process in police jobs and conducts extensive outreach programmes for this purpose.

It is necessary for the State Government to immediately prefer an appeal against this acquittal judgement with a view to ensuring that the accused persons get their just deserts and the wheel of justice grinds. One loud and clear lesson of Hashimpura is that the law enforcement officers as well as political leaders must realize that shocking miscarriage of justice, as seen in Hashimpura massacre, will erode faith of the minorities not only in the forces of law and order, but in the government itself. Instead of relying on major political parties and remaining in the political mainsteam, they will turn to narrow fundamentalist groups to represent their sectarian interests.

CHAPTER 3

Terror Attack at Pathankot

Just nine days after Prime Minister Modi's dash to Lahore, the terrorists from Pakistan belonging to Jaish-Muhammad outfit launched a vicious and violent attack on the Indian Airforce Station at Pathankot. About six to seven terrorists streaked across the international border into the air base. They waylaid a senior police officer, killed a cab driver and surreptitiously entered the IAF station at Pathankot. Their targets were the military assets at the air base. They intended to destroy the aircrafts and military helicopters stationed at the airbase. They were in touch with their handlers in Pakistan who were instructing them to blow up the aircrafts. Fortunately, they could not execute their evil design. They were neutralized and eliminated before causing any major damage. Security personnel, including a colonel from NSG, laid down their lives in countering the terrorist attacks. A large number of security personnel were seriously injured.

This well-planned attack by the trained terrorists belonging to Jaish outfit was meant to scuttle the new peace initiatives of Narendra Modi and Nawaz Sharif. It was hoped that the unprecedented gesture of the Indian Prime Minister of visiting Lahore will bring about a thaw in the tense and fraught relationship between India and Pakistan. It was also anticipated that the rogue and hawkish elements in Pakistan army and ISI will definitely try to create difficult and combustible situations to derail the peace process. This had been the pattern in the past and history has repeated itself.

It is a hard fact that many non-state actors and powerful elements in the Pakistan army as well as the ISI were feeling upset as the peace process between India and Pakistan gathered momentum. Talks between the two NSAs at Bangkok, followed by Indian External Affairs Minister's visit heightened their fears. Modi's sudden and surprise stop over at Lahore raised huge expectations and won approval from the people of both the countries. Terror leaders as well as the powerful elements in Pakistan army and ISI were feeling upset and wanted to put a brake on the evolving process. They felt that it was necessary to scuttle Nawaz Sharif's peace strategy and create a situation in which there will be a strong surge of public opinion in India against any peace dialogues with Pakistan. Modi Government will be under tremendous domestic pressure to call off further peace negotiations with Pakistan.

The key question that now arises is—whether the Pathankot strike had the overt or covert support of the all-powerful Pakistan army. The army is the real controller of the foreign policy in Pakistan, especially, towards India. It was anticipated that this time the army will be on board and it will back the peace initiative of Modi and Nawaz Sharif. Posting of General Janjua, a trusted officer of the Pakistan army chief, as the NSA strengthened the belief that the army also backs the peace initiatives of the two Prime Ministers. Narendra Modi took a risky decision knowing fully well that Nawaz Sharif is not the master of the house and peace with Pakistan is going to be a difficult and complicated process. There are both state and non-state actors influencing Pakistan's policy towards India and there is always the danger of sabotage by the "Deep State". Vajpai's visit to Lahore was followed by Kargil and Gurudaspur attack came in the wake of Ulfa declaration. Hence, some terrorist strike sponsored by Pakistan was not unanticipated after Modi's dash to Lahore. There is clear tell-tale evidence that the Pathankot attack had the clear signature of the ISI. This is also the view of the US counter terrorism expert Bruce Reidel, who feels that the attack was clearly meant to prevent any *détente* between India and Pakistan. The terrorists, as the telephone intercepts reveal, were talking with their handlers in Pakistan and receiving instruction.

Assessment of Foreign Ministry officials and experts was that after the Paris attack there was strong international opinion against those helping and harbouring the terrorists and abetting their acts of violence. This point was driven home to Pakistan Army Chief Raheel Sharif during his visit to USA. Developments in Afghanistan also were indicating signs of a change in Pakistan's policy. Pakistan knocked the bottom of its old Afghan policy by attacking North Waziristan and removing Afghan and Pakistan terrorists from its territory.

Pakistan's diminishing control over the Talibans has caused its loss of face before the USA and western powers. Afghan Talibans also no longer fully trust Pakistan. The proxy war against India no longer carries conviction among sections of people in Pakistan. Political parties of Pakistan are also in favour of peace with India. Hence, *jihadi* groups like Jaish, Lashkar-i-Toiba enjoying army patronage were keen to stall the peace talks and prevent any rapprochement between India and Pakistan.

However, it will be prudent to keep in mind that Indo-Pak peace negotiations will be a complicated and long-drawn affair and there should not be any unrealistic expectations. For success of any peace talks, Pakistan will have to make sincere and serious efforts to rein in the terrorists. This will need a paradigm shift in Army's perverse policy towards India and any such basic change in Pakistan Army's policy is not visible. However, calling off negotiations will only herald the victory of the terrorists whose main goal is to torpedo the peace processes.

India has now put the ball in Pakistan's court by linking foreign secretary level talks to Islamabad's prompt and decisive action against the attackers. Pakistan has been asked to act on the actionable intelligence provided to it by India. India has not imposed any deadline. The nature of Pakistan's response remains to be seen. It is unlikely that Pakistan will be able to initiate any decisive action against the non-state actors because it now clearly seems that the Army still remains opposed to any détente with India and pins faith in cross border terrorism. The army calls the shots and Nawaz Sharif wields very little control.

After the terror strikes, now post-mortem and blame game has started. The Defense Ministry has spoken of "gaps" in the security arrangement. There is criticism of the NSA Doval for deploying the NSG. Failure to quickly act on intelligence inputs has also invited criticisms. However, one must suspend the judgement before a thorough enquiry is done to unearth all the facts of the case. Any judgement based on available sketchy reports will be premature and one-sided. The fact, however, cannot be gainsaid that due to pre-emptive action on the part of the security forces, the aircrafts and other strategic assets could be saved. If these had gone into flames, there would have been a big loss of face for the government and intense pressure on it for quick, and perhaps knee-jerk, reactions.

Chapter 4

Unquiet Campus: Storm in JNU

Arrest and slapping of the charge of sedition against the President of the students' union of the Jawaharlal Nehru University by the Delhi police has provoked controversies and sharp criticisms of police action from different political parties, students' groups and academics. Action of the Delhi police has been held as highhanded, vindictive and authoritarian. Police action has been exposed to criticisms on various grounds. First, the charge of sedition under section 124(a) of the Indian Penal Code against the Union President will not stand scrutiny. Delhi Police Commissioner B.S. Bassi has said that the charge is not fabricated and the police have enough video and photo evidence to prove it. The case of sedition was registered on the strength of *prima facie* evidence. According to Section 124(a), a person commits sedition if he brings or attempts to bring into hatred or contempt or excites or attempts to excite disaffection towards the government established by law in India. It attracts the maximum punishment of life imprisonment.

Section 124(a) is a draconian provision enacted during the British Raj. Earlier, the Privy Council had made a literal interpretation of the section and held that any speech or writing which creates ill-feeling or disloyalty towards the Government could be viewed as sedition and a person guilty of such acts could be prosecuted and punished. But the Supreme Court, in its landmark decision in Kedarnath's case in 1962, held that just criticism of the government, though pungent and ill-informed, does not constitute an act of sedition. The apex court said that the sedition law would be attracted only if the offence was such that it would cause "public disorder" by acts of violence. There must be acts inciting violence and causing disturbance of peace and order. The court, however, held that the sedition provision in the penal code was constitutional. Hence, raising of slogans like "Pakistan Zindabad" and "long live Afghal Guru" and criticism of Guru's trial by the Supreme Court, though obnoxious and deplorable, do not come within the purview of sedition. It is alleged that the video footage showing the Union President raising slogans is a fake one. However, these are questions of facts to be decided by the court. It seems very likely that the charge of sedition may be thrown out by the court, causing acute embarrassment for Delhi police and then Government.

The second issue that has sparked off angry protests and comments is the passivity and inaction of the Delhi police when irate lawyers were running amuck in the court room of the Patiala House and beating up students, journalists and other sympathizers of the Union President. The Commissioner of Police has defended police action and said that the student leader Kanhya Prasad was not assaulted. He has also explained the difficulties of the police to arrest the lawyers inside the court and said that any effort to arrest the lawyers would have been resisted by the latter and turned the courtroom to a battlefield. From its long and bitter memory, Delhi police knows that physical confrontation with the lawyers is a risky proposition and would involve many of them in protracted departmental enquiries and court cases. Thus, some diffidence and caution on their part is understandable. Discretion trumped valour. But the correct and professional course of action on the part of the police would have been to film the lawless and violent acts of the lawyers and on the strength of the photo and video evidence start criminal cases and arrest these outlaws. This would have demonstrated that the police mean business and know when to draw the mailed fists out of the velvet gloves. Unfortunately, cases against the lawyers were not promptly registered. Further, cases were registered under bailable sections enabling some of the lawyers to get quick bails.

The police point of view that there had been no attacks on the students and journalists inside the court room has been negatived by the team of lawyers detailed by the Supreme Court and also the probe team of the NHRC. The NHRC team has unequivocally indicted the police and held that the attack on the students was—"planned and premeditated". There was serious security lapse on the part of the police. The investigating team of NHRC also said that the Union President Kanhya Prasad was subjected to psychological pressure and the statement issued by him owning allegiance to the Constitution was dictated by the police.

Available facts and evidence indicate that there was definite over-reaction on the part of the police while dealing with the students in JNU campus. The young students tend to be volatile and rebellious. They have to be tackled imaginatively and with restraint. A more nuanced approach would have defused the situation better. The USA had witnessed anti-Vietnam movements in campuses for nearly ten years from 1965 onwards, but there was no charge of sedition against any of the student leaders. Paris student turbulence in 1968 led to change of the Government, but none thought of framing sedition charges against the students. It appears that police action was to a certain extent influenced by extraneous influences and pressures. In any tense situation, the senior police officers should take into account the surrounding circumstances and make their own independent assessment and not get influenced by the dictates of others. This brings into focus the urgency of police reforms to insulate the police from extraneous political pressures.

The National Police Commission in its Fourth Report (1981) has recommended that the police should have good knowledge about the campuses in their jurisdiction and remain acquainted with the problems therein. In order to achieve this objective, where there is a large concentration of students, the police should constitute a Special Cell, comprising carefully selected officers to deal with such situations. This is a practical recommendation which should have been acted on by the Delhi police. In any academic institution, the primary responsibility of maintaining peace and discipline in the campus is that of the academic authorities and the police should come in the picture only when there is serious breach of peace. Unnecessary interventions and resultant confrontations will blur the image of the police in the minds of the students and the community at large.

Some protagonists of the ruling party have expressed the view that the JNU should be closed as it has become a hotbed of left-leaning students and teaching staff airing anti-national views. Any such course of action will be shortsighted and self-defeating. This will only amplify the image of student agitators and expose the Government to national as well as international obloquy.

CHAPTER 5

Will-O'–the–Wisp of Police Reforms

The issue of police reforms is agitating the minds of many police officers for a long while. When we joined the Indian Police Service in the 60s, one constant refrain of our discussions was the creeping politicization of the police and the woefully inadequate resources and infrastructure of the police force. Another constant irritant was the control exercised over the district police by the Collector as enjoined by the police manual. Some of my erstwhile colleagues and friends openly fell out with the District Magistrates and others maintained an uneasy equation. Most of the political leaders and Ministers at that time used to treat the senior officers of the police with some respect and did not interfere in day-to-day police administration. But they would unblushingly assert their authority and control whenever their political interests were involved.

The situation started gradually changing with the passage of time. Ministers and local MLAs, particularly, of the ruling parties, became more assertive and abrasive and started demanding postings and transfers of the officers of their choice in suitable police charges and dabble in the investigation and prosecution of cases to help their cohorts. Senior police officers also for getting suitable postings and continuing in greener pastures started first bending and then crawling before the politicians, and particularly, the Chief Ministers who in most of the states held charge of the police.

I still recollect an incident in early 60s, when in an open police conference, the then Chief Minister of Orissa, roundly and very unkindly lambasted the police for its all-round failure in law enforcement and order maintenance and other acts of omission and commission. We squirmed in our seats but the head of the police force (at that time IG of Police) remained silent and petrified in his chair. But the Chief Secretary of the state, an ICS officer of outstanding caliber, took up the cudgels on behalf of the police and pointed out that some of the critical comments of the Chief Minister were unmerited. This kind of plain speaking has now become history. IAS and IPS officers now cower before the Chief Minister and never dare to contradict him.

The Police Act of 1861, has remained unchanged because the political leaders, who suffered at the hands of the police before Independence found it convenient like their colonial masters to have a police totally subservient and at their beck and call. The National Police Commission (better known as the Dharamvira Commission, 1978-81) recommended for the first time some bold and positive steps to insulate the police from extraneous political pressures and pulls so that it can function as people's police and not ruling party's police. In Prakash Singh's case, the apex court (2006) issued seven point directives including setting up of State Security Commission, fixed tenure of the DGs of Police and Police Establishment Board etc. Unfortunately, no state has so far implemented these recommendations and directives and resorted to various stratagems to scuttle them. Some of them enacted police Acts which are far more retrogressive than the Act of 1861. The apex court has so far refrained from pulling-up the errant State Governments despite the report of the Justice Thomas Committee which pointed out deliberate non-implementation of the apex court's directives by different states. Years have rolled by and the issue of police reforms remains stuck in doldrums.

Against this determined opposition of the politicians of all hues, the fate of police reforms remains uncertain. Another hurdle is that the police house is not fully united and galvanized in championing these reform proposals. Many police officers in the field, particularly those of subordinate ranks, remain unenthused and also do not feel that the proposed reforms will help them in their work, and enable them to function with greater dignity. They also remain unconvinced that police leaders will adequately safeguard their interests. Indeed, the cause of police reforms will continue to suffer setbacks unless the police leaders can convince their junior colleagues that the proposed reforms will insulate them from the political influence and enable them to function with greater efficiency and satisfaction.

Public support for police reforms also remains lukewarm. Members of the public, even the enlightened ones, feel that without some political control the police will turn into a rogue elephant and misuse its power and authority. It will run amok. They forget that the unshackled police will also have to function under rules and laws circumscribing police authority and scope for misuse of power. They will be hauled up before the courts for acting contrary to laws. They will never be omnipotent. Under the present arrangement the police officers can enjoy considerable immunity and unaccountability if they can keep the political masters in good humour. This has become the be-all and end-all for many police officers and is playing havoc with police administration. The responsibility of upholding people's rights and standing by them in their weal and woe is relegated to the background. This is detrimental to public interest and snaps the chain of command and control in the police. In order to win public support, the police have to be more transparent, accessible, conscientious and honest. Instead of opposing formation of Police Complaints Authority, as recommended by the National Police Commission and directed by the Supreme Court, police leaders should welcome it and urge State Governments to establish such control mechanisms early. Police reforms also should go beyond the directives of the court and embrace measures that will win public support. Community policing initiatives by enterprising police officers have not been successful in many states because of the unwillingness of the police officers to share authority with the public and allow citizens an important say in the framing of police policies and operations. A citizen centric police reforms is the crying need of the hour.

Hence, a time has come for a careful reappraisal for fashioning correct strategies for police reforms. In the face of dogged resistance from the political masters, only reliance on apex court's directives alone will not work. Steps have to be taken to harness the support of the public as well as a subordinate police staff for the cause of police reforms which brook no delay. Only then the movement will gather momentum and compel the political masters to unshackle the police to function in accordance with the rule of law and not by the rule of politics. A neutral apolitical and efficient police functioning in accordance with the rule of law will help the cause of good governance and public welfare.

CHAPTER 6

Community Policing: Rhetoric and Realities

Community policing has become a buzzword not only within the police, but across societies and communities worldwide. It is practiced in many forms and with different results in many countries of the world. However, practices which are defined as community policing vary widely. There is lack of conceptual clarity regarding community policing even among the police officers. Some hold the erroneous view that any kind of contact between the police and community come within the domain of community policing. Some of the key concepts of community policing are thus lost sight of. In reality community policing implies changing the concept of the role of the police in the society. It involves a paradigm shift from the traditional view that police alone can reduce crime and disorder and it accords a significant role to the community in defining and guiding the police in their locality.

The main aim of community policing is to break down the anonymity of policing and diminish the psychological distance between the police and the community by "*putting faces in uniform*". The key elements of community policing include community-based crime prevention, practice of service as opposed to emergency response, shifting of command responsibility to lower ranks and public participation in planning and supervision of police action.

A survey of community policing in the USA and some of the western countries show that "*professional policing*" model of 1960s and 70s which relied on up-to-date technology in police work and insulation of the police from political influence had its own innate shortcomings. Technological advances were reducing police contacts with the public as the police spent more time in hi-tech equipped cars and rise in crimes, especially in inner cities, went unabated. Community policing emerged as the police recognized that their tactics were not reducing crime and were in some cases contributing to civilian disturbances. It was felt that the public should play a more active role in promoting order and safety. The police cannot bear the responsibility alone. Though community policing is first and foremost a crime prevention effort, it does not mean cessation of police efforts to detect crime, arrest and prosecute offenders. Successful community policing is expected to improve and enhance other police operations by increasing community's cooperation with the police.

There is a facile assumption that community policing means that the community wants closer partnership with the police. Very often this is not the case. There is lurking skepticism of the community that the police are not serious and look upon this as a public relations exercise. To win community's confidence and trust, the police will have to demonstrate that they sincerely seek community's help in combating crime and disorder. There is also fear of the public that they may have to face reprisals from the criminals if they closely cooperate with the police.

It has been noticed that there are some definite obstacles in implementing community policing programmes. One of the major implementation challenges is the resistance of police officers to community planning.

Police unions internationally view community policing as a threat to police professionalism. They feel that the police are the appropriately trained agency to control crime and in this work the citizens are neither needed nor wanted. Further, community policing also requires some kind of police accountability to the community and this is not acceptable to police unions who fear loss of jobs and benefits. Obstacles also come from the police sub-culture where display of authoritarian use of force is appreciated. In community policing however the police have to play a problem solving parental role.

One of the common criticisms of the community policing programme is that they do not make police more responsive to the community rather they increase police control over the community. Community policing has been practiced in varied degrees of success in many countries in the world.

Community policing experiments have been implemented successfully in countries like Japan and Singapore. In Singapore successful functioning of Neighbourhood Police Centres (NPCs), have enabled Singapore police to provide better and efficient services to the community. Community partnership has provided police with invaluable insights and inputs and enabled it to refine police responses to law enforcement problems. In USA, there has been massive federal support for implementation of community policing programmes, but the American experience in community policing suggests that the programme has not always resulted in reduction of crime, but made the community less fearful of the police.

In India many enterprising police officers have experimented with various community policing programmes, but most of them had not been very successful because they failed to elicit support of the people. The members of the public felt that police are pussyfooting and not serious on community's support. For example police have taken various steps from time to time involving community and seeking their help in controlling crime and disorder, but an assessment of community policing practices of Delhi Police conducted by a scholar of Police Research and Development found that the members of the public were neither impressed nor enthused by the operations of the community policing initiatives. Many of the respondents drew attention to the lack of interest of police administration in involving the public in implementing community policing schemes. The police fear public interference in police work. Police personnel interviewed on the other hand blamed the public for their apathy and alienation from the police.

Some community policing experiments like the formation of *mohalla committees* at Bhiwandi in Maharashtra have been uniquely successful in preventing communal disturbances. In respect of community policing initiatives in India, it is seen that the success of rural based community programmes unlike the urban programmes, has been limited. There has been an urban-rural divide. There has also been a lack of continuity. The unhealthy predecessor successor syndrome has also neutralized the positive effect of good work done by some energetic officers. There has also not been adequate training of personnel entrusted with the responsibility of community policing which represents not a small technical shift in policing, but a paradigm change in the way the police operate.

CHAPTER 7

Plight of the Undertrials: Failure of the Judiciary to Set Things Right

Actor Salman Khan's conviction and sentence of imprisonment for five years and his quick suspension of arrest and granting of bail by the Bombay High court raises serious concerns about the criminal justice system of the country. It also sends a clear and chilling message that our courts are prompt in giving relief to the rich and the powerful and callous in delivering justice to the poor and disadvantaged. Salman Khan's case dragged on for 13 years and at the end of the day the convicted accused without spending an hour in prison went home and soon also got the bail from the court. His able lawyers must have marshalled powerful arguments, but the fact remains that only a rich man engaging the best legal brains can overawe the courts. The whole episode only strengthens the public perception that scales of justice in our country are always tilted in favour of the rich.

Again Salman Khan's case is to be juxtaposed against thousands of undertrials languishing in jails without getting bails. According to Prison Statistics, India's total number of jail inmates is now about 3.8 lakhs of which 2.54 lakhs are undertrials who constitute about 66.84 per cent of the prison population. This has had a very deleterious impact on prison administration. Majority of the undertrials are poor people with rural and agricultural background and they are languishing in prison because nobody is there to bail them out. They are also not in a position to provide sureties. In prisons they live cheek by jowl with convicted prisoners in violation of the provisions of the Indian Prisons Act and Jail Manuals. In some prisons there are separate wards for the undertrial prisoners but essential facilities like hospitals and kitchens are common. So, it is not at all possible to maintain segregation between undertrial and convicted prisoners. Lodging undertrial prisoners with the convicted prisoners lead to "contamination of crime". Many callow and inexperienced young men coming in contact with hard boiled criminals get coarsened and criminalized. It is known that many of the gangsters recruit members of the criminal gangs out of these borderline yet redeemable offenders admitted in jails. Further, constant movements of prisoners in and out of prisons facilitate smuggling of narcotics and other contraband articles. Again most of the undertrials go without any work or training and spend time in depressing idleness. All India Jail Manual Committee better known as Mullah Committee strongly recommended that there should be separate institutions for accommodating undertrial prisoners and they should be located near the court premises to reduce the problems and hazards of transporting the prisoners.

Overwhelming preponderance of undertrial prisoners causes overcrowding in jails. While working in NHRC, I have visited prisons where more than 90 per cent of the prisoners were undertrials. In the United Kingdom, the report on prison disturbances by Lord Wolf highlighted the knock-on effect of overcrowding on prison administration and their baneful impact on the minds of the prisoners. According to the report very often a substantial number of prisoners leave prisons "*more embittered and hostile to society than when they have arrived*". A report submitted to the Punjab and Haryana High Court on the plight of undertrials in Bhatinda Jail in Punjab revealed that whenever a new entrant comes he is deployed to cleanliness duties and to discharge from that duty Rs. 500 to Rs. 100 are charged.

There are a number of reasons for the gross and inordinate delay in the release of undertrial prisoners. The most important of them is of course judicial apathy. The prisoners are in judicial custody and they continue to languish in jails because cases against them drag on interminably in courts of law. According to the Supreme Court's dictum bail and not jail is the right of the individual and in Hussainara Khatoon's case (1979), the apex court interpreted that the right to life and personal liberty under Article 21 of the Constitution includes the right to speedy justice including the right to free legal aid. Unfortunately, the ground realities are different. The District Legal Aid bodies headed by District and Session Judge have singularly failed to provide legal aid to the undertrials. Research shows that quality of legal aid is poor and lawyers in some cases were reported to be demanding money from the poor inmates. On an average, an undertrial takes 5 to 6 months to get bail and there are cases where it had taken 1 to 4 years for the prisoners to be bailed out. It is also a fact that it is the poor prisoners who suffer and the rich ones are able to get bails quickly.

The National Human Rights Commission has drawn attention of the Chief Justices of the High Courts to the delay in granting of bails to undertrial prisoners and suggested a number of remedial measures. One of them is that as the prisoners are in judicial custody the District judges should regularly visit the prisons within their jurisdiction and identify cases of long-staying undertrials which need special attention. It is also recommended holding of special courts in jails and its monitoring by the Chief Justice/Senior judge of the High Courts. The Commission further recommended monthly review of the cases of the undertrials in the light of Supreme Court's judgement in the case of Common Cause *vs*. Union of India (1996). In this judgement, the Supreme Court had given clear directive for release on bail and discharge of certain categories of prisoners specified in the judgement. However, these recommendations and exhortations have made marginal difference in the situation. Even the amendment of CrPC in term of Section

436A which provides that when a prisoner has undergone detention for a period extending up to one half of the maximum period of imprisonment specified for that offence, he shall be released on his personal bond with or without sureties. The section also provides that in no case an undertrial prisoner should be detained beyond the maximum period of punishment for which he can be convicted for the alleged offence. The Supreme Court in a PIL has now directed the trial court judges to visit jails, identify undertrials who have done half of their sentences and release them on bail with or without sureties. Many prisoners are languishing in jails for years for petty offences. After Supreme Court's directive, it was hoped that there will be relief for the undertrial prisoners. Unfortunately, this has not happened. Due to lack of technology and coordination, the maximum period of detention of prisoners in jails is not computed properly. Further, many judges want to leave the grant of bail decisions to High Court to avoid allegations. Thus, jail and not bail continues to be the norm, particularly in respect of poor and disadvantaged prisoners. Judicial apathy is largely responsible for this distressing situation.

Chapter 8

Avoidance Syndrome

Way back in 1969 well-known police scholar, David Bayley in his seminal book "*Police and Political Development in India*" had written that in India, police-public relationship is characterized by a powerful "avoidance syndrome". Members of the public try to avoid as far as possible any contact with the police and this avoidance syndrome is more pronounced in the northern parts of the country than in the south. Even now a fair amount of fear and distrust between the police and the public persists everywhere in the country. Different studies and surveys confirm this conclusion.

Some time back a bottom-up assessment of the Karnataka police titled "*Mirror of the Police*" was done by Public Affairs Centre, Bangalore. The survey showed that for the Indian police, time has stood still and the public trust and confidence in the police have not registered any improvement. A powerful avoidance syndrome is still at work. In this survey 2500 complainants from different walks of life all-over the state as well as 500 police personnel were interviewed. Interviewed police personnel comprised inspectors, sub-inspectors, head constables, constables and writers. One of the major findings of the study was that a significant section of the public does not feel "at ease" in dealing with the police. This is mainly due to the psychological barriers that have persisted over the years and continued unchanged. This avoidance syndrome is more pronounced among the complainants belonging to scheduled tribes and scheduled castes and other marginalized sections of the society. Most of them are also illiterates. The prevalent police culture of disrespect for human rights of the downtrodden perhaps explains this phenomenon.

A significant number of complainants (45%) also stated that they do not get any information from the police regarding the status of their complaints. Any such information is furnished only after repeated visits to the police station (as mentioned by 64% of the complainants). This is an all-pervasive malady witnessed in police organizations all-over the country. Police seldom take initiatives to inform the complainants of the status of the complaints and steps taken by the police so far in the investigation and detection of the case. Many police officers attribute this failure to the pressure work or inadequacy of staff. This does not reflect the truth. The real cause is perhaps the lack of police culture to be proactive as well as helpful to the complainants. Our police officers forget that even small proactive gestures are appreciated by the members of the public and go to enhance the image of the police in public mind.

Corruption of police officers during registration and follow-up investigation of cases surfaced during interaction with the complainants and interviewing of the police officers. Though many complainants did not admit payment of bribes to the police to get the work done, many others were under the impression that they were not paying bribes, but investigation expenses incurred by the police to which they must contribute. Some of the reported purposes for which extra amount was demanded and paid included payment for conducting enquiries speedily and nabbing the accused persons. Incidentally, a large number of persons who paid the bribes said that their work was not completed even after payment of bribes. This accentuated their bitterness. Another, disturbing aspect of the situation was difference between the complainant's version of the complaint and description of the case recorded in the file. In short, prolonged complaint lodging process and poor follow-up action left the complainants, by and large, dissatisfied. Their first encounters in many cases with the police were not happy ones.

Dr. Bayley's study of public perception of the police shows that unflattering views about the police are more readily found with individuals who have had unfavourable contacts with the police. Familiarity breeds contempt. Though the survey showed quick closure of a number of cases during one year, a fairly large number of cases dragged on for a long time. There is no doubt that timeliness in closure of cases and a positive and helpful attitude of police will enhance the complainants' satisfaction and improve their perception about the police.

Surveys done earlier at the instance of the National Police Commission (1978–81) have unveiled that unpleasant contacts with the police create a negative image of the police in public mind. People who have had the experience of the police misconduct or misbehaviour are more prone to believe that police frequently misbehave.

Feedbacks received from the police personnel who had been interviewed showed their loyalty to their department and satisfaction with the job which enable them to render help to the members of the community. But they expressed disapproval of the rigid hierarchical structure of the police organization, and difficulties in freely communicating with their senior officers, who have a tendency to take credit for the work done by their junior colleagues.

The nature of the job also fuels their anger and frustration. Most of them are hard pressed and hard-worked. They work for 15-16 hours a day and often are not given the leave which is their right (64% reported never getting a weekly off). However, Karnataka police authorities have done well in providing necessary infrastructure at the police station. For police officers in the field, the job-related stress and strain is compounded by a pariah feeling which makes many a police officer demoralized and cynical. The police occupation is accorded low esteem, esteem accorded is much lower than the importance of function discharged by the police.

The job-related stress and emotional overload causes, in the words of the behavioural scientist Christiana Maslal "burn out" in many officers. Like a wire that has too much electricity flowing through it, the officer just burns out and emotionally disconnects.

Many of the complainants, particularly those who are poor and illiterate, remain unaware of their legal rights and do not complaint of their rough rude treatment by the police. For improving police response it is necessary to spread legal awareness among the public. This should be one of the foremost functions of civil society and human rights groups.

Another interesting point emerging out of the study was that there was a contrast between the satisfaction levels as indicated by the police personnel as opposed to the satisfaction level of the complainants. Only 47 per cent of the complainants indicated satisfaction with their interaction with the police. Satisfaction level of the police personnel was much higher (80%). But the satisfaction level will drop sharply if the views of those who failed to get their cases registered by the police are taken into account. This indeed is the main challenge before the Indian police leaders. People in general understand and appreciate constraints of the police and do not expect detection of all their cases and redressal of every grievance. They appreciate if the police are sympathetic and positive. Citizens' satisfaction will be higher when their complaints are promptly attended to at the police stations level and they receive a copy of the FIR. Though satisfaction level has an element of subjectivity, the study shows, that quality of service is the key determinant.

CHAPTER 9

Adieu to Death Penalty

Death penalty enjoys strong public support in India. There is broad public perception that death penalty deters crime and is needed to curb serious acts of crime and violence. In Bacchan Singh's case (1980), the Supreme Court after surveying considerable literature on the subject concluded that death penalty has some deterrent impact. But this viewpoint is being challenged by many criminologists in different parts of the world. In a consultation on capital punishment recently organized by the Law Commission many jurists and academics pointed out how public opinion over this issue is based on misconceptions about the alleged deterrent impact of death penalty. In 1945, Travancore was an independent state in India and did not have the death penalty. 962 murders were committed during the years 1945 to 1950. When Travancore became a part of India and death penalty became applicable to the state, there was an upswing in the rate of murder. Similarly, the homicide rate in Canada was 542 in 2010, which was 159 less than the homicide figures of 1975, the year prior to the abolition of death penalty in Canada. In the United States also some of the states that have the death penalty, homicide rates are higher than in the states that have abolished it.

Criminological studies have also shown that death penalty does not alter criminal behaviour and only prevents rehabilitation. More than severity of punishment, it is the certainty of punishment that acts as a deterrent. In Bacchan Singh's case, the apex court further observed that *"real and abiding concern for the dignity of the human life postulates resistance to taking human lives through law's instrumentality"*. It held that death penalty can be imposed only in the *"rarest of rare cases when the alternative option is unquestionably foreclosed"*.

Notwithstanding the ruling of the Supreme Court, death penalty in India extends to a variety of offences. Under the Indian Penal Code death penalty can be applied to a variety of offences like murder, gang robbery with murder, abetting the suicide of a child, waging war against the government. Death sentence also can be imposed for a number of offences committed by members of the Armed Forces under the Army Act (1950), Air Force Act (1952), Navy Act (1956). The Sati Prevention Act (1987), makes death penalty applicable to individuals convicted of abetting a successful *Sati*.

Correct statistics on execution within India are not available. The number of people executed in India since 1947, remains a matter of dispute. Official statement claim that only 52 people had been executed since Independence, but People's Union for Civil Liberties (PUCL) quoted information from Appendix 34 of 1967 Law Commission's Report that 1422 executions took place in 16 Indian states from 1953 to 1965. The Government instead of responding to PUCL's discovery has maintained silence. India, however, had been observing a *de facto* moratorium in execution since 2004, but in 2012, Azmal Kasab was executed for his involvement in Mumbai carnage (26/11). In 2013, Afzal Guru was hanged for a terror attack on Indian Parliament in 2001.

Error in Judgement

The possibility of error in judgement is a powerful argument in favour of abolition of death penalty. Like all other forms of punishment, the error in judgement cannot be ruled out in the case of death penalty. Until a decade ago the prevalent view was that such errors of judgement are historical oddities and could not be repeated in modern times. In USA, several studies have documented the problem of erroneous conclusion even in homicide cases. In USA, the Report of Death Information Centre (1999) documents that since 1970 there have been nearly 80 people released from death rows as they were found innocent. Execution of an innocent man is an unpardonable crime against the society and such gruesome possibilities cannot be ruled out in case of imposition of death penalties.

A landmark study titled "*Lethal Lottery —Death Penalty in India*" carried out by Amnesty International and Peoples Union of Civil Liberties (PUCL) highlights the weaknesses in the award of death penalties in India since 1950 and observed that death penalty in India has been "*arbitrary, imprecise and an abusive method in dealing with crimes and criminals*". This report has been referred to by the Supreme Court in a number of cases.

Arbitrariness

Even the Supreme Court in the case of Swami Shraddhananda *vs.* State of Karnataka (2008) held that awarding the sentence of death depends a good deal on personal predilections of the judges comprising the bench. This indeed is a serious admission on the part of the apex court. It is well-known in legal circles that all-over the world each court has some "*hanging judges*" and life and death of a person can become a matter of chance, depending upon which bench of the court hears a particular case. In the case of Sangeet *vs.* State of Maharashtra (2013), the apex court admitted that death penalty was wrongly imposed in five other cases and added that uncertainties in India's "*death penalty jurisprudence*" makes it difficult to decide whether the case was fit for imposition of the death penalty.

During the apartheid regime South Africa was one of the world's greatest executioners of the world. South Africa's

Constitutional court in a landmark judgement declared death penalty unconstitutional mainly on grounds of arbitrariness. The court further concluded that "*poverty, race and chance play roles in the final decision as to who should live and who should die*".

In its dissenting judgement in Bacchan Singh's case Justice Bagawati observed that death penalty has a class complexion and caste bias. Now, a study conducted by National Law University students with the help of Law Commission analyzed data from interviews of 373 death row convicts over a 15 year period and found that three fourth (3/4) of those given the death penalty belonged to backward classes and religious minorities. Very often poor people get a rougher treatment from the courts because of their inability to find a competent lawyer to contest their conviction.

Today there is an international tide in favour of abolition of death penalty. The number of abolitionist nations has risen to 104 of 196 UN member states and a vast majority of them has abolished death penalty for all crimes in all circumstances including terrorist offences and crimes committed in time of war.

In India many of the death row prisoners have had to wait for considerable period in prisons under sentence of death. Indeed, death sentences have no penological value and execution serves only a symbolic purpose. India has not signed the International Covenant on Civil and Political Rights, Second optional protocol, aiming at Abolition of Death Penalty adopted by the UN General Assembly in 1988. In 2007, India voted against the United Nations General Assembly Resolution for a moratorium on death penalties.

There is an imperative need for a strong civil society movement against the death penalty in India. The point must be stressed that those who favour the death penalty do not conform to the opinion held by a majority of people in the world which is veering towards its abolition. The question of death penalty is a basic human rights issue and a litmus test for all states proclaiming human rights norms and values. Gallows stand for cruelty and irreverence for life.

Chapter 10

Jihadi Terrorism Haunts Europe

The spectre of *Jihadi* terrorism is now haunting Europe. The multiple bombing attacks at Brussels International Airport and the Molenbeek Metro Station demonstrated that Islamic State (IS) has spread its tentacles successfully in different countries of Europe. It has set-up a number of sleeper cells in different European countries and can activise them as and when necessary. It can draw on supporters some of whom have bomb-making ability and can communicate securely. They use encryption for their electronic communication. Just as the French authorities had no advance intelligence regarding the Paris carnage on November 13, 2015, the Brussels attacks also came as a big surprise to the Belgium authorities. They were caught napping.

Salah Abdesalem, the master planner behind Paris attacks, was on the run for a long time. It was known to the police authorities that he has travelled back to Belgium, but it took two months for the Belgian police to get some clues and arrest him with an accomplice. The long period of time Abdesalem was on the run shows that there are groups and contacts to support and shelter him and they are embedded in broader communities and neighbourhoods.

In the aftermath of Paris attack considerable attention was focused on problems such as disenfranchisement and segregation as well as the radicalization of the Muslim communities in different countries of Europe. Most of the migrants came from former colonies with linguistic affinity and were absorbed in low-end jobs, which were acceptable for that generation in search for better lives. But their next generations are better educated and unwilling to follow their predecessors footsteps. Many of them are unable to find better jobs. They feel angry and frustrated. The migrants are mostly from Islamic nations which have helped groups such as Daesh to establish networks amidst them. Daesh attracted recruits on the basis of slick advertising and returned many of them back to Europe who have now become part of the sleeper cells all-over the European cities. The level of preparedness of the cells is evident from the fact that it took not more than 5 days to launch their revenge attack after the capture of Abdusalam at Brussels where headquarters of European Union and NATO are located. It seems that the terrorists have acquired the capability to launch devastating attacks on a regular basis in different cities of Europe. There are reports that London can be the next target of serial bomb attacks and such attacks can be against soft targets with the aim of causing as many casualties as possible. The Brussels attack took the predictable course of targeting the softest targets any urban centre offers—the transport system. Metro infrastructure can hardly be protected and its targeting produces spectacular results for the terrorists.

The tragic events in Brussels and Paris will no doubt raise questions regarding interstate intelligence cooperation, refugee policy and eventually the whole project of European integration. Many European countries have dealt in the past, though not very effectively, with the problem of terrorism. The Irish Republican Army (IRA), the Italian Red Brigades (IRB), the German Baader Menhof group had limited capabilities and avoided most of the times civilian casualties. But now the game has changed and the terrorists are targeting the civilians without any hesitation or compunction. The IS aims at the repetition of "Spanish Scenario" that is the electoral defeat of politicians who favour military action against the militants as it happened with former Spanish Prime Minister Jose Marias Azner following 2004 Madrid bombings. Scenzen passport free zone should have suggested the need for joined-up intelligence long ago. Unfortunately, that has not happened. Inter-agency cooperation is poor. Europol, the law enforcing agency of the EU does a useful job in facilitating information and analysis, but it has no executive powers to carry out investigations and works on a low budget. It is doubtful if Europe can act in a way that America did in the aftermath of 9/11. It was quickly understood that failure of different agencies to pool and share intelligence had been responsible for the catastrophic attacks. America through the agency of Homeland Security had so far succeeded in preventing another serious attack on its soil. It is an indication that the lessons were learned well. In Britain also, the British police with its experience of combating IRA terrorism over decades have so far succeeded in warding off devastating terrorist strikes.

There is every likelihood that Paris and Brussels attack will reignite anti-Muslim sentiments in Europe. It will also have an impact on Europe's political future as well. The successes of anti-refugee party Alternative fur Deutschland (AfD) in the German regional elections have proved that Europe is facing a crisis of confidence and may slip into a new era of intolerance and nationalism. In Finnish Parliament election in 2015 the ultra right the Finns Party scored 17 per cent of votes, the Neo-Nazi Golden Dawn gained 7 per cent in the Greece Parliamentary election, an unprecedented high percentage of votes for a country that suffered havoc wrought by the Nazi, during the Second World War. Indeed, the combination of economic stagnation, intense refugee flows and *jihadi* terrorism would become a game changer for European domestic politics. The ultra right will exploit the events in their bid to gain power through elections. Attacks in Belgium will intensify debate about BREXIT. Though the British Government has wisely maintained control over its borders, there is considerable concern among the British public regarding border security in the SCHENGEN zone and unregulated migration. A BREXIT would intensify ethnocentrism across the continent and increase Marine Le Pen's chances of winning the French Presidency in 2017.

CHAPTER 11

Taliban Strike again in Pakistan

Violent Taliban attack on prestigious Badshah Khan University in Khyber Pakhtunwalih province of Pakistan has once again demonstrated that Tarikh-e-Taliban (TeT) is down but not out, and they are capable of wreaking havoc by devastating terrorist strikes. They had earlier killed more than 130 school children by launching an attack on the Army Public School in Peshawar. They have now again threatened to attack more schools all-over Pakistan. Taliban commander Umar Mansoor has justified the attack on the schools and colleges by saying that students from these institutions join the army and the government. But another Taliban spokesman condemned the attack and called it un-Islamic, showing perhaps a possible split among the embattled Pakistan Talibans. Pakistan authorities have said that the Talibans operating from inside Afghanistan in Pakistan-Afghanistan border area were responsible for this outrage. Some conspiracy theorists in Pakistan have also pointed accusing fingers at the Indian intelligence agencies and dubbed them as the facilitators.

Under the present Pakistan Army Chief Raheel Sharif, Pakistan had embarked upon a serious counter-terrorist offensive in North Waziristan, which had become a haven of the Talibans. There was significant success. Many of the areas, so long under the control of the militants, have been retaken by the state. A number of Taliban commanders were killed during the army operations. The army had also launched a big drive against the terrorists and criminal elements in Karachi. Due to the operations of the army, the militant violence has marked a perceptible decline during the last 10 months in Pakistan and Raheel Sharif has become a popular hero.

After being pushed out of Northern Waziristan, the Pakistan Taliban leaders, under Mullah Fazlullah are operating from Afghanistan. Because of ideological affinity, Pakistani Talibans are receiving support from the Afghan Talibans and thus it will not be easy for the Pakistan army to completely overcome and overpower the Talibans. It is sucked in for a long-drawn campaign. Pakistani Talibans have claimed that they are in possession of indigenously developed missiles. Some rogue elements in Pakistani army may have helped them in this regard. Hence, Pakistan army is constrained to cultivate and keep in good humour other non-state, India-focused actors like Jaish-e-Mohammad (JeM), Laskar-e-Toiba (LeT) Frankansteins, created by the Pakistani army, and to ensure that they do not join hands with Pakistani Talibans and turn against the state. Hence, chances of Pakistan government, despite international pressure, tightening the screw on them are remote.

Jaish is a banned organization, but it has been allowed to operate without any let or hindrance in Pakistan. Jaish has cells, which have links with Al-Quaeda and Afghan Taliban. After a long hibernation, its leader Azhar Masud has emerged on the scene when in 2013, he addressed a huge rally of his supporters in Muzaffarabad over phone and called on Pakistani authorities to lift all restrictions over *jihad*. Nawaz Sharif government's action to detain Azhar Masood and arrest a few other JeM operatives is a cosmetic exercise with a view to pleasing USA and the international community. There are reports suggesting that a number of NATO countries considered the intelligence supplied by India to the Pakistan authorities after Pathankot attack as credible, if not conclusive evidence. A repeat of Mumbai stand off would expose Pakistan to ridicule and bring it under international pressure, including threat of sanctions. But Pakistan security establishments are neither willing nor prepared to go for a crackdown on the JeM.

Similarly, Lashkar-e-Toiba (LeT) is a India-specific group nurtured by the ISI. At present, ISI has control over it and it is siding with the army in its confrontation with the Tarikh-e-Taliban (TeT). So, the army is unwilling as well as unable to come down heavily on these non-state actors. Unfortunately, Pakistan army is failing to realize that the LeT has wider ambitions. It is adherent to the principle of Sunni Wahabism and its aim is to establish universal Islamic Caliphate and recover all lands that were once under the Muslim rule. These objectives are very much akin to that of the Al-Quaeda and also of the Islamic state (Daesh). At present, it is under the control of the ISI which permits it to raise funds by various dubious means. Its founders, Hafiz Saeed, Abdullah Azam, Zafar Iqbal have larger ambitions and will not play second fiddle to the "Deep State" indefinitely. If the Pakistan army seriously tries to control and defang them, they will, like Afghan Talibans (TeT), stir up troubles and join hands with the enemies of the state. The Pakistan army has failed to appreciate the aphorism of Hillary Clinton that the snake at the backyard will bite not only the neighbours but sooner or later turn against the master.

Pakistan is facing, as Jessica Stern mentioned in an article in Foreign Affairs, a typical principal-agent problem. The interest of Pakistan (Principal) and those of the militant groups (agents) are not aligned. It was hoped that the Pakistan army and the ISI were on board with Nawaz Sharif and backed his initiatives for a détente with India. But Gurdaspur, followed by Pathankot attacks, show that army's agenda has not changed. It will not allow Nawaz Sharif to wrest control over the foreign policy, particularly, policy towards India. Destabilizing India by thousand cuts remains an obsessive motive of the Pakistani army and it is not going to change soon. The world knows, and many in Pakistan also realize, that the fear of existential threat from India is a phoney fear intended to bolster army's position as a protector of country's integrity. Asraf Qazi, former Pakistan ambassador to USA, India and China, has perceptively written in an article in Dawn (January 12, 2016) that if the rulers of Pakistan "convey the message that they are unwilling or unable to control cross border activities of anti-Indian and anti-Kabul *jihadis* unless Kashmir is solved and Kabul has a friendly government, they will do more harm to Pakistan than any enemy could wish for".

President Barak Obama has now sent a stern message to Pakistan and urged it to delegitimize, disrupt and dismantle the terrorist networks operating within its territory. It is doubtful how far Pakistan will listen to it and what amount of pressure America will be able to exert. America needs Pakistan's help in stabilizing Afghanistan and hence will not dare to exercise tough measures. India has to bear all these realities in mind while engaging with Pakistan. It has to keep in mind the option of a robust response if any further likely terrorist attack from Pakistan materializes. The civilian democratic government in Pakistan is in favour of better relations with India is partly true. The political military and bureaucratic elite which rules Pakistan, though there may be some differences among the constituents, share a deeply adversarial perception of India. This is a hard reality which has to be always borne in mind.

Chapter 12

Fall Outs of Brussels Attacks

The multiple bombing attacks at Brussels International Airport and the Molenbeak Metro station, which killed 30 people and injured many, demonstrated that the Islamic state has spread itself successfully in different countries of Europe and can draw on supporters, some of whom have bomb making ability and can communicate securely. Just as the French authorities had no actionable intelligence as to what was to unfold on November 13 in Paris. Brussels attacks, similarly came as a sudden surprise to the authorities. The terrorists apparently used encryption for their electronic communication.

According to many, it was a revenge attack after the capture of Salah Abdesalam, the master planner behind Paris attacks. It was known to the police authorities that Abdesalam has travelled back to Belgium after the Paris attacks, but it took months for the Belgian police to get a lead and capture him with an accomplice. It was clear that a number of sleeper cells are operating in Belgium and Abdesalam's arrest may have been a trigger to them to go into operation with a plan that may have taken weeks or months in preparation.

It is possible that those responsible of carnage at Brussels wanted to strike before the security agencies acted on any information divulged by Abdesalam, who is known to have backed out of a suicide attack. The conspirators feared that he may cooperate with the authorities. Belgium's Foreign Minister Didier Reynders had said that Abdesalam have told investigators that his group was planning an attack on Brussels. In that event, there was clear failure of the security agencies to foil a known threat. The long period of time Abdesalam was on the run shows that there are groups and contacts to support him and provide him with necessary shelter. They are deeply imbedded in broader communities and neighbourhoods.

Belgium has now become one of the nerve centres of *Jihadi* terrorism in Europe. Almost 500 Belgium citizens have travelled to Syria and Iraq to fight on the side of the Islamic state, making Belgium the biggest known supplier of foreign *jihadi* fighters. A group called Sharia-4 led by a charismatic preacher Fouad Belkasem was actively involved in recruiting the foreign fighters.

In the aftermath of Paris attack lot of attention was focused on problems such as disenfranchisement and segregation as well as radicalization of the migrant Muslim communities. Belgium has migrant population of 26 per cent and 8 per cent of the total is Muslim and their number is increasing. Molenbeek, an area north of Brussels, has emerged as an area of concern where a large number of Muslims coming from former colonies have settled down. Most of the migrants accepted low end jobs which were acceptable to that generation in search for better lives. But the better educated next generations find it difficult to follow the footsteps of the earlier generations. They feel angry and frustrated when they are unable to find better jobs.

They find themselves at a disadvantage at the job market. They speak only French and Arabic and many jobs require knowledge of French, Flemish and Dutch and sometimes English. Arrival of funds from Saudi Arabia and other Persian Gulf states in 1970s facilitated setting up of conservative schools in the areas. A decade ago Belgium journalist Hind Frahihi went undercover in Molenbeek and wrote a popular newspaper series that showed that disillusioned young Muslims were being influenced by radical preachers.

It is among these groups Daesh has established its networks and attracted young recruits through slick advertising. Many of them have returned from Iraq and Syria and have been used for extensive sleeper cells that can be activated as and when necessary. The level of preparedness of the cells is evident from the fact that it took not more than 5 days to execute the vicious armed retribution in the heart of Europe where headquarters of European Union and NATO is located.

Two Ministers, Interior Minister Zan Jambon and Justice Minister Koen Jeens offered their resignations at a cabinet meeting. The Prime Minister Charles Mitchel declined to accept it. At a special session of Belgium Parliament Jeens laid blame on the door of the police services for not identifying the airport bomber Ibrahim EL Barkraoui despite warning from Turkey.

Europe is now confronted with a hard reality that IS has acquired the capability to launch devastating attacks on a fairly regular basis. There is report that the London Police and the British Army's specialized forces are seriously apprehending that the London can be next target of serial bomb attacks and such attacks will be against the soft targets with the aim of causing as many casualties as possible.

It is not certain if Europe can react in the same way America had done after 9/11. In America it was quickly understood that the failure of different intelligence agencies to pool and share intelligence was responsible for failure to prevent the devastating attacks of 9/11. Stringent security measures fashioned by Homeland Security helped America to prevent further serious terrorist onslaughts. In Britain too with the experience of combating IRA terrorists for decades the security agencies have successfully so far warded off terrorist onslaughts.

There is every likelihood that Paris and Brussels will reignite anti-Muslim sentiments in Europe. There is real concern that nationalist movements across Europe will use the fear of more terrorist attacks to force mainstream political parties to adopt some hard-line measures against Muslim migrants. Without doubt Europe faces a long term threat of terrorist attacks. It will have to deal with them from security point of view as well as socially and politically.

Chapter 13

Halt in the Onward Advance of ISIS

It seems that the tide of war is gradually turning against the Islamic state of Iraq and Al-Sham (ISIS) and its advance which at one time appeared unstoppable has been halted. With the capture of Mosul from the Iraqi army last June, the ISIS had been able to acquire a huge stockpile of arms and ammunitions supplied by America to Iraq – armoured vehicle, anti-tank and anti-aircraft missiles, fleet of Humvees and vast quantities of ammunitions. In its campaigns, the *Jihadis* of ISIS demonstrated their capacity to launch successfully a hybrid warfare that fuses terrorist and insurgent techniques with conventional warfare. They have also shown their capacity to launch complex operations simultaneously in Syria and Iraq. One of the successful tactics of ISIS has been to first soften the targets with heavy artillery fire and then open breaches with suicide bombings and follow it up with attacks with Humvees fitted with guns from all sides. Speed, willingness to suffer casualties coupled with savage treatment of the prisoners, scare the defenders to flight.

ISIS now occupies a vast area of Syria and Iraq, an area of the size and population of Jordan. It is estimated that it has more than 30,000 fighters in fray. Its strength is also augmented by a large number of foreign *jihadis*. In January, the International Centre for Study of Radicalism and Political Violence—a London based Think-tank—estimated that at least there were 20,000 foreign *jihadis* surpassing the number that came to defeat the Soviets in Afghanistan in 1980s.

President Barak Obama has given the call for "degrading and ultimately destroying ISIS" and 60 odd countries have now joined the America-led coalition. The coalition is training Iraqi government forces and providing arms to Syrian and Iraqi Kurds. The ground situation shows that ISIS is no longer able to advance in areas where the Shias and the Kurds are in majority. ISIS forces failed to capture from the Kurds Kobanni, a Syrian town on the borders of Turkey. After 4 months of grim fighting, the Kurdish fighters with the assistance of coalition bombers have succeeded in overcoming this seize by the ISIS forces and expelling them. About 1000 ISIS fighters were killed in this prolonged operation. ISIS also remains paranoid about the local population under its control and fears that they may switch sides. This explains why it seeks brutal expulsion of moderate Sunnis and other minorities from the areas controlled by it.

It is also getting financially hit. Areal bombings have destroyed many oil installations and ISIS earnings from sale of oil have plummeted about two thirds from $ 2.3 million dollars in June 2014 to about $ 1 million a day now. Banks under its control have run out of cash. The income from ransoming of hostages has also come down. By ransoming the hostages, it raised about $ 20 million in 2014. Though ISIS remains a rich terror group, it is a poor state. Its claim to rule and usher in a glorious Caliphate is eroded by poor governance and service delivery.

But in order to effectively degrade and destroy ISIS, America will have to give up its policy of "no boots on the ground". Obama has now asked the Congress for a fresh authorization of the military force (AUMF) endorsing limited use of ground forces including ground troops against the Islamic state and its allies. There are already some 2630 American troops in Iraq, advising Iraq and Kurdish forces and protecting American installations. Domestic polls in USA show that after the murder of the American aids worker Kayala Mueller, American public now view ISIS as a serious threat to its security, but are not in favour of sending ground troops if air strikes fail to provide expected results.

Now, a plan for big offensive by Iraqi and Kurdish forces to recapture Mosul which has a population of about 1 million people and was captured by ISIS in last June is afoot. Pentagon views this a "pivotal battle" where US advisors will be on the ground near Mosul to direct close air support. There are some hard-nosed militarists in USA who advocate the view that America with its allies must interfere in a big way to defeat the *jihadis* and occupy the heartland held by them. It will have positive spin-offs. A Caliphate without territory will lose its legitimacy and appeal and fail to attract the *jihadis* from all corners of the globe. A Caliphate, unlike Al-Quaeda, cannot go underground. ISIS leader Bagdadi has already called himself "Commander of the Faithful", a title reserved for the Calipha only. But the risks of escalation are very high. Direct American intervention will provide an enormous propaganda victory to the ISIS. It will also add fuel to the suspicion that America wants a modern-day crusade to kill Muslims. This will go to encourage worldwide recruitment of the *jihadis*. It seems that the present American strategy to bleed ISIS through areal bombings and proxy war is the best military option under the circumstances. Without expansion, ISIS will lose its magical appeal and become like any other Middle-Eastern Muslim state that has failed to improve the lives of the people. The land it controls, though vast, is poor and undeveloped, and when stories of miseries and sufferings of the people staying there start circulating, the appeal of ISIS will definitely weaken.

Difference with Al-Quaeda

Jihadism sometimes is mistakenly viewed as a monolith. In reality this is not the case. Terrorism has evolved and taken different forms, colour and dimensions. There are some clear differences between

Al-Quaeda and ISIS. ISIS disdains Al-Quaeda's priorities and has no respect for its current leadership. They view Al-Quaeda's leader Zawahari as ineffectual. Bin Laden tried to organize geographically diffused autonomous groups in different countries of the world to carry out terrorist activities. By contrast, Islamic state needs a territory to remain legitimate as well as a top-down structure to rule it. It is also hobbled by its own ideology which may be proved to be its undoing. The present international system is premised on the willingness by each state to recognize its borders but any such recognition by Islamic state will tantamount to an ideological suicide. The Caliphate has not border and has to continually expand. Accommodations and negotiations are viewed as acts of apostasy and not credible options.

A few "lone wolf" supporters of ISIS have on their return attacked western targets and have been cheered by the Islamic state. But so far ISIS has not planned or financed any such attack. The attackers are by and large amateurs. "Charlie Hebdo" attack in Paris in January was an Al-Quaeda operation. ISIS immediately has no appetite for terrorist operation, in distant countries. They are concentrating on expansion in neighbouring areas and consolidating their rule in occupied areas.

The end of the Islamic state, however, is not going to come about soon. A successful operation against ISIS will only be practicable when they can be eliminated from their heartland in Eastern Syria. Fighting the terrorists is infinitely harder when they enjoy a haven. But in Syria continuance of the Assad regime creates a serious problem. Earlier Assad acquiesced in the expansion of the ISIS, Sunni tribes in Syria who had previously fought against ISIS are unwilling to join hands with pro-Assad forces. A political solution to the Syrian war is necessary to effectively contain the ISIS. Further, things can go wrong if the Islamic state can come to an understanding and win the allegiance of Al-Quaeda, though at present there is a wide rift between them. This is at one stroke will expand the unity of its base and make it a terrible foe.

CHAPTER 14

Caliphate is Bouncing Back

The Islamic Caliphate of Iraq and Syria is striking back. After the capture of Tikrit, home town of Saddam Hussain, there was optimism in government circles in Iraq and amidst American-led coalition forces that the advance of ISIS has been halted. The Prime Minister of Iraq Al-Abadi triumphantly declared that the IS is on its way out. Now, the fall of Ramadi, the capital of Anbar province of Iraq, and the humiliating rout Iraqi forces has altered the picture and shown that such optimism was misplaced. Iraqi army fared no better than when it fled Mosul and left behind large quantities of military hardware. Ramadi fell when a wave of suicide attacks by IS soldiers punched through its defences. Ramadi was the last city held by the government in the Sunni dominated areas of Iraq. IS now menaces Baigi oil refinery and the power plant at Baigi on which Bagdad depends. The news of capture of Palmyra in Syria by IS has further heightened alarm in Bagdad.

As the battle rages in Iraq it is becoming clear that, despite heavy American bombing, IS has remained unbowed. US Secretary of State Chuck Hegel while briefing the Congress on US mission in Iraq and Syria said that after heavy American air strikes, IS has changed its tactics and adapted itself well to the new ground situation. It is operating in small groups making it difficult to identify the targets and also camouflaging the heavy ammunitions. *Jihadi* groups have described their tactics in colourful phraseology, "We are like serpents among the rocks slithering here and there".

German journalist Jurgen Todenhofer who had visited Mosul after its capture from Iraqi forces writes that the IS is much stronger than what the west believes. It is receiving unlimited supply of volunteers with high morale from different countries of the world. It is a fact that IS has suffered reverses in the war. Its territory has shrunk and air raids have damaged many of the oil installations under its control and its revenue has slashed. Some of its commanders including its deputy leader have been killed in air strikes but this has not dampened its morale. It is resolutely pushing forward in the Sunni regions of Anbar province. Many of the disaffected Sunni groups marginalized by the Shia-led government of Iraq are joining hands with them and swelling their ranks.

The problem before the Iraqi Prime Minister is that the Iraqi army has proved to be a paper tiger. The incompetent Iraqi generals have recruited ghost soldiers and lined their own pockets. They take to their heels whenever a crisis situation erupts. Unable to rely upon the Iraqi army, the government has turned to the Shia militias for help. But this may prove to be a double-edged sword. Reliance on Shia militias will exacerbate Shia-Sunni tension in the region. There is also the lurking danger that if the Shia militias who have now assembled for recapture of Ramadi emerge victorious, they may challenge the authority of the wobbly Iraqi government. The Shia militias have code named their Ramadi recapture operation as "Labiak Hussain" a slogan in honour of the grandson of Prophet Mohammad killed in the battle that led to the schism between the Shia and Sunni Muslims. America has described the code as "u helpful" as this will antagonize the majority of the Sunni population of the Anhar province.

Now, to stem the tide of ISIS advance, a more robust American response is called for. America alone has the power and technical know-how to roll back the IS advance. There are hard-nosed US strategists who espouse the view that America should directly intervene and reoccupy the vast swathes of territory overrun by IS. Caliphate without territory will get delegitimized and cease to attract followers. But this may prove to be a wrong and risky venture and provide a propaganda opportunity to the IS to portray America as an inveterate enemy of Islam. But Obama's policy of "no boots on the ground" has to change.

President Obama has called IS capture of Ramadi as a "tactical setback". But it is far worse than that. American strategy of bleeding ISIS to death through aerial bombing is not working. Senator John McCain, Chairman of Foreign Relations Committee, has said that 70 per cent of American air attacks failed because targets could not be identified. Hence, American soldiers and experts have to be embedded in the Iraqi army to improve the accuracy of the air strikes. Special commando operations of the type which killed IS leader Abu Sayyaf have to be launched and Iraqi army, has also to be provided with more ammunitions and "logistic assets", so, they do not run out of ammunition and get butchered. After the fall of Ramadi, the US Defence Secretary Ash Carter said that the will to fight is missing in Iraqi army. Shia-led and Shia-dominated Iraqi army had displayed unwillingness to fight for Sunni dominated territories in Anbar. Iraqi government is unwilling, even after American goading, to arm the Sunni tribes who earlier under American tutelage were instrumental in clearing out the Al-Quaeda from Anbar. This antipathy of the Iraqi army towards the Sunnis and the latter's reluctance to cooperate with the army has further complicated the troubled situation.

Meanwhile, IS is trying to win the hearts and minds of the Sunnis in the areas overrun by it. Decapitation notwithstanding, they have set-up a fairly firm and efficient administration. Salaries of the soldiers and public servants are being regularly paid. It is becoming clear that the Caliphate is not disintegrating and it will be increasingly difficult and time-consuming to oust it from the areas under its control. Overthrow of IS is possible only when it is dislodged from its heartland of Syria. But this will not happen till the regime of President Assad in Syria continues. The Sunni tribes of Syria who had earlier fought against the IS are unwilling to join hands with Pro Assad forces. Thus, some sort of *de facto* partition of Iraq has taken place with the IS entrenched in north-west, Kurds in the north-east and the Shia dominated government in control over the south. One does not know when, if ever, IS dominated areas will come under the control of Iraqi government.

Another forbidding development is that many terrorist groups proclaiming allegiance to IS have sprouted in different countries. IS supremo Bagdadi had openly proclaimed the intention of ISIS to expand eastwards to establish the Islamic Caliphate of Khorasan which will include Afghanistan, Central Asia republics, Iran and Pakistan. However, at present IS is fully preoccupied in Syria and Iraq and terrorist attacks in America, Australia, and Paris were "lone wolf" operations. It is also seen that Al-Quaeda, despite its doctrinal differences with IS, is changing its strategies. It no longer wants to remain autonomous conspiratial groups, operating in shadows in different countries. It is trying to follow the agenda of IS. In Yemen it already rules over large expanse of territories. There is the ominous possibility of IS and Al-Quaeda joining hands and widening the base and range of their operations. This will make the IS a terrible foe.

Now, Australian Foreign Minister Julia Bishop has warned that IS groups have collected radioactive materials from hospitals and research establishments in cities it has captured in Syria and Iraq and is capable of making "dirty bombs". It may also smuggle nuclear weapons from Pakistan to attack US. It is not known how far this kind of alarmist view based on reports of Australia's defence department is correct or exaggerated, but it indicates the threats IS poses to the civilized world and highlights the need for collective action against this international scourge.

Chapter 15

Afghan Quagmire

The US military forces in Afghanistan have started preparing to handover the responsibility for security to Afghan soldiers and the police by the end of 2014. The drawdown has already commenced. The US President, Obama says that this will mark the "responsible" end of the war in Afghanistan. Unfortunately, this is not going to be so. Though the active presence of US troops may end, the war in Afghanistan is likely to continue and it is difficult to predict at this stage the ultimate outcome. A prolonged civil war is likely and this will create in its train a host of security and strategic problems for the entire region. The earlier tough talk *vis-à-vis* the Taliban is now replaced by plans to allow it a say in Afghanistan power structure.

The US hopes that after the withdrawal of its troops, the Afghan National Army would take charge of the situation and hold its own. The performance of the Afghan National Army so far had been inconsistent. It may be able to hold its own against the forces of Haqquani network and the Mullah Omar forces of Quetta Sura as long as the US Congress pays the multibillion dollars annual bills to keep the force fighting. In the year 2013, the Afghan National Security Forces' operating budget was to the tune of $ 6.5 billion—more than twice the Afghan government's entire federal revenue. Most of the money has to come from the United States and it would be difficult for an American President to defend the Afghan end whenever instances of killings of American advisors occur or when the Afghan President makes sharp and critical references against America. Indeed, it takes time and great deal of money to build-up an efficient army.

Further, ongoing negotiations with the Talibans are going to be prolonged and complex. Some have doubted if the Talibans are at all serious about negotiations. Time is on their side and America is fixated on a early exit. After all in late 2011, the Talibans assassinated Bashiruddin Rabbani, the head of President Karzai's Peace Council who was entrusted with the task of moving the talks forward. The Talibans can wait, wear down the Americans and win an outright victory. But the truth of the matter is that Talibans are also interested in the negotiations as that will provide them a source of legitimacy. Again, they do not form a monolithic group and are divided into many factions who do not always work in close coordination. And some of them are seeking agreement with the Americans. Mullah Omar and other leaders of Taliban factions living in Pakistan for a decade are feeling constrained and restless and willing to strike a deal. Taliban leaders are also in constant dread of assassination by US drone attacks. They would prefer a settlement if it does not amount to a capitulation.

Pakistan feels happy at the turn of events. For its safe exit and meaningful negotiations with the Talibans, US is very much dependent upon Pakistan. Pakistan has given up blue-sky ambitions for a Afghan puppet state under Taliban domination. There is also growing realization in Pakistan that peace in north-western Khyber Paktoonkha province and the federally administered areas is impossible without a peaceful settlement in Afghanistan. Pakistan's main interest is to ensure that any future Afghan government does not become an Indian ally. This is Pakistan's close-to-worst nightmare. It seeks to prevent Afghan-Indian axis that could threaten it.

According to reports from Afghan officials, Pakistan seems less paranoid about India these days. Its greatest concern is the terrorists at home who are viewed as Pakistan's greatest security threat. "The Pakistan Taliban" says Ahmed Rashid are in no mood for talks. They are sitting on their high horses expecting the state to surrender. But there is a danger that elements in Pakistan army wedded to *jihadi* proxies may be tempted when American troops are withdrawn to direct some of the groups towards India, risking further conflicts between the two neighbours. Present Prime Minister Nawaz Sharif, despite well meaning pronouncements and gestures, may not be able to prevent it.

America's negotiations with the Talibans are going to be prolonged and complex. Any further settlement in Afghanistan will have to grant the Talibans a political foothold. The foothold would not give them control of the government, but the legal status would allow them electorally and expand their position later. Unfortunately, the bigger problem in Afghan scenario is the misgovernance of Karzai government. President Karzai's administration has been corrupt and shambolic. The Talibans though brutal, are seen as incorruptible whereas Karzai's administration is corrupt and exclusionary. The fear is that if Kabul's misgovernment persists, a brutal but honest opposition will make headway. Though Karzai will not be eligible to contest the election in 2014, he would want a successor who will secure his interests. If the elections are rigged, the way they were in 2009, it would damage the political transition of the country after the US pulls out.

China is also quietly seeking access to Afghanistan's rich oil and mineral resources. China's National Petroleum Corporation has won rights to exploit and develop oil fields in Amudarya basin in Afghanistan which has enormous oil reserves. China will not like the prospect of a prolonged civil war in Afghanistan which will prevent it from fully reaping the benefits of its investments.

For India, the end game in Afghanistan will pose a very serious foreign policy challenges. India disagrees with the prescription that the Talibans will become a regular political party and will not seek to overwhelm the government. Afghanistan is of great strategic significance for India. If however, a full-fledged civil war breaks out India's strategic alliance with Afghanistan will spawn problems. There are strategists who are of the view that besides providing arms and equipments India should put its troops in the ground to prevent a hostile Taliban takeover. But dispatch of troops on the ground will raise hackles in many quarters and will require a robust national consensus which will be difficult to obtain in present coalition-based politics. There is always the danger that strategic alliance with Afghanistan may become an albatross round India's neck.

Chapter 16

Confronting the Islamic State

In his address to the nation after the terrorist strikes in Paris, President Barak Obama vowed to destroy the Islamic state which is spreading the poison of terror and violence all-over the world. Earlier, while sanctioning airstrikes against IS he had declared that America would "degrade and destroy" the IS, but the progress in this respect has been agonizingly slow. Bombing missions by the US and its allies have now been joined by France and Russia. Air strikes to some extent have affected IS operations and stopped its advance, but not seriously affected its fighting capacity. Pentagon sources claim that coalition strikes killed about 2000 IS fighters in the 14 months since their onset in 2014. This may be an optimistic assessment, but there is no doubt that a number of *jihadi* commanders may have been killed. Michael West, an American journalist, was told by an IS defector that during the intense bombing in Koban, a Kurdish enclave in Northern Syria, more than 2000 IS *jihadis* perished. Further, tightening of the Turkish borders has made it difficult to replace the fallen IS fighters. This is one of the reasons prompting IS attacks on "far enemies" with the calculation that such attacks will be force multipliers in propaganda terms, but the fighting capabilities of IS have not been seriously dented. According to the CIAs estimate, the groups manpower ranges from about 30,000 to about 1,00,000. Further, IS fighters are far more dedicated and disciplined than their Iraqian and Syrian counterparts. For the recapture of Tikrit, numerically stronger Iraqi forces were kept at bay by smaller stubborn IS defenders. Willingness to use Kamikaze tactics does give IS fighters an edge, but they have also displayed sound tactical skill and fire discipline.

IS has changed tactics and adapted itself well to the ground conditions. It is operating in small groups, which makes it difficult to identify them. It is also camouflaging its heavy arms and equipments. Intense bombing of urban areas where IS *jihadis* are mainly based is causing considerable unintended collateral damage to the civilian population. Further, urban areas surrounded by buildings make drone operations very difficult.

IS is also a financially strong terrorist organization. According to estimates prepared by American and European officials, IS earns about 1 billion dollar a year from sale of oil, ransom and forcible collection of taxes. After the capture of Mosul, it plundered the banks whose vaults contained an estimated 424 million dollars. IS Caliphate now includes some of the best agricultural lands in the Fertile Crescent and the heavy industry that Saddam Hussain had concentrated in the loyal Sunni areas. A report compiled for Reuters in 2014 lists 13 Iraqi oil fields, 3 refineries, 5 cement plants and 1 salt mine under IS control. Its revenue system has so far proved largely impervious to sanctions and air raids.

Killing of some of the top commanders crippled Al-Quaeda's operations in many places, but mere eliminating some of the leaders may not be of much help in the case of IS. IS has set-up a pseudo-state complex administrative set-up, which though not a model, is functioning and would carry on even if Amir Al Bagdadi and his two prominent lieutenants Abu-Ali-Anbari and Abu-Al-Turkmani do not remain on the scene.

After terrorist strikes in Paris, France has stepped up air strikes in a big way and it has also taken the lead to solve the differences between US and Russia. But despite all the battering IS endures. Its territory remains one of the safer parts of Syria and many civilians from neighbouring areas have sought shelter there. What is more important food is cheaper and there is justice of sorts. It doles out alms to the poor in exchange of total obedience. It has also built a personality cult around Bagdadi and churns out turgid propaganda through social media to attract foreign volunteers. Indeed, IS has used social media far more effectively than any other terrorist groups. It has successfully exploited the anger and frustration of the disenfranchised Sunnis. Its apocalyptic view of the final battle ending in the triumph of the Caliphate has made it attractive to many angry and disenfranchised young men seeking adventure and violence. End of IS will not be possible unless it is dislodged from the territory it holds. It uses the territory to raise and train thousands of terrorists from all-over the world. Its capital Raqqa has become a "New Jerusalem" for the *jihadis*.

In USA, there are mounting pressures on Barak Obama to send ground troops to drive out the IS from the territories held by them. A Caliphate without territory will lose its legitimacy and its appeal will gradually wither away. It will not be able to attract *jihadis* from all corners of the globe. Al-Quaeda, cockroach like can go underground but Islamic State cannot. Without its grip on occupied areas of Syria and Iraq it will cease to exist. But dangers of escalation are very high and any such move will be welcomed by IS. It will add fuel to the suspicion that America and western nations want a modern day crusade to kill Muslims. This will also encourage and facilitate worldwide recruitment of the *jihadis*.

After Paris, the mission to "degrade and destroy" has acquired far greater urgency. The present plan of American-led coalition to train and equip the Iraqi and the Kurd forces to do the fighting and throw out the IS may not ultimately succeed. The policy of "aggressive containment" has not so far worked. Iraqi army's performance on the ground thus far has been quite disappointing. Efforts have to be made to see that the existing plan works by providing more trainers and special forces to work with the Iraqi units. But if that plan does not work troops have to be brought from outside to throw out IS from the territory it occupies.

But successful action in Iraq will be possible only when the problem of the continuance of Assad regime is resolved. French President has suggested a common front with Russia and putting up with Assad to continue the fight against IS. But the problem is that Assad and his militant Iranian supporters are sworn enemies of the Sunnis whose homeland is the IS territory. Obama is still reluctant to deploy ground troops, but demand of such a course of action will mount with new waves of attacks on the West threatened by IS. A violent large scale attack on American soil will settle the debate in the form of direct action.

But there remains the baffling problem of holding a war-ravaged hostile territory after the IS is overthrown. Iraqi forces are overstretched and deeply disliked by the Sunnis whom they want to liberate. But breaking up of the Caliphate will not snuff out the appeal of IS and its malevolent ideology. It will continue to fester in many collapsed and failing states stretching from Algeria to Pakistan. Different groups professing IS ideology will sprout and spread venom. The world will have to live with this nightmare for a long time to come.

CHAPTER 17

Crying Justice

Recently, while addressing the conference of the Chief Ministers and Chief Justices of High Court, the Chief Justice of India made an emotional and almost tearful plea for appointment of more judges to resolve millions of pending cases in the courts across the country. This will, he said, do justice not only to the poor litigants, but also restore confidence among the foreign investors, whom the government is trying to attract.

It is a fact that the number of judges in the country is totally inadequate to cope with the staggering pendency of cases in different courts. The cancer of pendency of cases and consequent delay in their disposal has crippled and paralyzed the criminal justice administration in the country. According to PRS Legislative Research Report 32 million cases (civil and criminal) are pending in courts and out of them 58,000 cases are pending in the Supreme Court and 42 lakh in various High Courts and 2.8 crore cases in sessions and subordinate courts. Pendency of cases has increased in last 10 years in the Supreme Court by 148 per cent and 53 per cent in High Courts. The fact cannot be gainsaid that increase in the number of cases is not matched by an increase in the number of judges. There are 10-12 judges per million people in the country while in advanced countries there are 50 judges per million. The apex court is itself running short of its required strength by 6 judges and 464 vacancies exist in various High Courts.

However, increase in the number of judges, though urgently necessary, is not the only answer. Some urgent institutional and systemic changes are called for. The critical test to be kept in mind is not the judge-population ratio but the judge-docket ratio. Docket refers to the list of cases to be tried and is an accurate indication of the work load of a judge. In India, the docket ratio per judge for proper and minor matters is 987 whereas it is 3235 per judge in USA. The answer perhaps lies in effective court management, which unfortunately so far has not been seriously attempted by the Indian judiciary.

The Arrear Committee headed by late Justice V.S. Malimath set-up in 1990 identified the various causes of accumulation of arrears in the High Courts. According to the Committee, some of the causes are: (a) litigation explosion; (b) inadequacy of the staff attached to the High Courts; (c) inordinate concentration of work in the hands of a few members of the Bar; (d) lack of punctuality among the judges; and (e) inadequate supply of the copies of judgments and orders etc.

The Law Commission as well as the National Police Commission in their reports had suggested various measures that can be applied to reduce the huge backlog of cases in the courts. Some of the immediate steps that can be taken without delay or difficulty are: First, a large number of petty cases, particularly, under the different sections of Motor Vehicles Act form a big bulk of pending cases for want of appearance of the accused persons and witnesses, who get dispersed after detection of the offence. There should be ticketing system for on-the-spot disposal of the trafficking offences, which will help in a big way reduction of cases pending for trial in the courts. Second, there should be periodic review at different levels of every police case pending in the court for more than one year from the date of filing of the charge sheet. A decision should be taken whether it will be in public interest to continue with the prosecution of the case. For example, in property offence cases, in which the first offenders are involved or cases where the value of property is less than Rs. 500. Such cases should be considered for withdrawal with the consent of the complainants. The Law Commission in its 154th Report (1996) endorsed the recommendation of the National Police Commission and said "the periodic review of the pending cases can be undertaken with a view to striking many of them out from the court's calendar".

Adjournment

There is, very often, unacceptable and avoidable adjournment of cases both at the stage of trial, appeals and remissions. Though Section 301 CrPC provides for holding of the trial proceedings as expeditiously as possible, it is an open secret that there is enormous delay in the disposal of cases because of frequent adjournments. When the sessions trials begin it must be heard day to day till the end. Non-availability of witnesses or counsels should be no ground for adjournments. Indeed, pursuit of perfection in courts has led to near-collapse of the system. None can ensure complete justice and the objective of the court should be that the system must work. The Law Commission in its 154th Report recommended that every criminal court shall send a return in a prescribed proforma to the Chief Justice of the High Court stating the particulars of the cases in which adjournments were granted by them during enquiry or trial of cases with details thereof.

It is a matter of regret that the courts in the country have, by and large, remained untouched by the management revolution of the twentieth century and information revolution of the present century. Computers have not been used successfully to improve court management. There should be provision of e-filing in all the courts, starting from the sessions and above. All judgements and records should be uploaded online. Court notices, summons in petty cases, service of documents to be made online wherever possible. These steps will go to reduce delay, corruption and result in eradication of misplacement of files. It is unfortunate that though

India is a leader in information technology and BPO service, our courts still use bullock cart facilities in this age of supersonic speed. Instead of focusing only on the increase in the number of judges, the courts should be equipped with modern technology and amenities to facilitate quicker disposal of cases. It may be mentioned here that a judge in America in this respect has a definite edge over his Indian counterpart. He is provided with a suitable staff of law clerks, paralegals to assist him in the management of files, and research and analysis of evidence.

At present, a vast number of old and outdated laws clutter the statute book. Earlier an exercise undertaken by the Central Government had shown that over 1200 central laws were either to be amended or repealed. It is a pity that most of the State Governments have not undertaken this exercise to identify laws that have no utility and should be repealed. According to a survey, almost two-thirds of the civil cases in courts are directly related to land and property matters.

Today, of the three branches of the state, judiciary is still held in respect by the people. But there is gradual erosion of public respect for the judiciary for a variety of reasons. The main danger to the judicial system is from within. Bad appointments and poor supervision are taking their toll. NJAC controversy highlighted the need for transparency in the appointment of the judges and rejigging of the collegium system. A former justice of the Supreme Court, Ruma Pal has aptly said that the "process by which a judge is appointed to a High Court or elevated to the Supreme Court is one of the best kept secrets of the country". The judiciary must also discourage frivolous pubic interest litigations and seriously reconsider about continuing with the practice of long court vacations, despite criticisms from all quarters.

Chapter 18

National Human Rights Commission: A Critical Overview

Constitution of the National Human Rights Commission in 1993 marks a watershed in the annals of the Human Rights movement in the country. Protection of Human Rights Act (PHRA) created a high-powered Commission to be headed by a former Chief Justice of India for protection and promotion of human rights in the country. A retrospective analysis after more than two decades since its inception shows that the Commission's record of performance is somewhat mixed. It has done a laudable job in creating human rights consciousness in the country and sensitizing public servants and political authorities over many issues concerning human rights. But its record is uninspiring in many other spheres of its work and over the years, there has been a steady decline of its credibility. Many a civil society groups (at times unfairly) have become critical of the Commission. The Commission's recommendations also do not always receive serious attention from the Government.

A combination of external and internal factors has been responsible for gradual erosion of NHRC's credibility and effectiveness. Some of the infirmities of the Commission are embedded in the Act itself. PHRA gives NHRC only recommendatory powers. It cannot issue judicially enforceable orders giving rise to criticisms that it lacks teeth. A high powered Commission should be vested with some authority to enforce its decisions. The Commission is totally dependent upon the government for its manpower and financial requirements. Regarding choice of personnel, its field is narrowed to what is made available by the government. Further, due to lack of in-house training facilities and programmes, it fails to sensitize and reorient its staff to their new role. No wonder, NHRC over the years, has acquired the image of a bureaucratic organization.

Section 19 of the PHRA further emasculates the NHRC and prevents it from enquiring into violation of human rights by the armed forces, which include within its ambit the central paramilitary forces. The Commission, thus, cannot enquire into egregious violations of human rights in the insurgency-affected areas in Kashmir and the North-East.

The Commission receives large number of complaints regarding various kinds of violation of human rights. The number has swelled exponentially over the years. From the lowly figure of 169 in 1993-94, it shot up to 1,06,990 in 2012-13. This speaks of the growing credibility of the Commission and the yearning of the people for trouble-free expeditious justice. The Commission has awarded compensation to the victims in a large number of cases and also ensured that its recommendations in this regard are complied with. But it has failed to ensure that errant and truant violators are visited with condign punishment. Again disposal of a large number of complaints *in limine* continues to cause disappointment and frustration among the complainants. Reasons for *in limine* disposal should be clearly indicated and explained to the complainants. A more victim-centred responsive approach should replace a formal and legalistic one. The Commission is becoming a victim of its own formalism. Though complaints against the police comprise bulk of the complaints, the complaints against the armed forces are few, constituting less than 1 per cent of the total complaints filed before the Commission. This is perhaps due to the perception in public mind that the Commission exercises limited control and jurisdiction over the armed forces.

The NHRC has urged state police authorities to open human rights cells in police headquarters. This body will take steps for human rights training and sensitization of police officers and men. NHRC also refers many cases of complaints against the police to the human rights cells at police headquarters. Unfortunately, most of these centres have become dysfunctional and NHRC has failed to galvanize them.

NHRC has pressed the State Governments for setting up of State Human Rights Commissions (SHRCs) in keeping with the provisions of PHRA. Unfortunately, over the years, many of the SHRCs have become dysfunctional. PHRA makes each SHRC an independent entity with very little supervisory control exercised by NHRC. Moreover, the Act stipulates that NHRC cannot enquire into any matter pending before a State Commission. This provision has been used by scheming violators to avoid an inconvenient forum and getting the complaints filed before a forum of their choice. NHRC had earlier set-up a Committee under Justice Ahmadi, a former Chief Justice of India, to suggest amendments of the PHRA with a view to enhancing the effective functioning of the Commission. But the major amendments of the Act proposed by the Committee to remove some of the impediments hampering efficient working of the Commission were not accepted by the government, reflecting disregard for the Commission's autonomy and constitutional legitimacy.

The prestige and credibility of the Commission to a large extent depend upon the public respect for the Chairman and members of the Commission. The NHRC had during the period of more than 20 years some outstanding Chairpersons and members respected for their probity and knowledge, but there were also members, who viewed their jobs as sinecures and took lukewarm interest in their work. Ahmadi Commission recommended that the Chairperson of the Commission should be a member of the appointment committee so that his views in the selection of members could be taken into consideration. The recommendation was not accepted by the government and thus the Chairperson has no say in the choice of the members. Appointment of some members of the Commission as state governors in the past dented the independent image of the Commission.

The NHRC however, has a number of landmark achievements to its credit. It has played a transformative role in creating human rights consciousness in the country and preventing wanton violation of human rights by public servants. It has displayed laudable initiatives in taking *suo moto* cognizance of important human rights concerns like police reforms, prison reforms, child labour, bonded labour, custodial death and torture. It showed great courage and commitment by taking *suo moto* cognizance of the communal holocaust in Gujarat and indicted the State Government for its failure to firmly control it. It also brought to the centrestage social, economic and environment rights of the people and highlighted their importance and relevance in the universe of human rights.

Experience of National Human Rights Commissions in different countries of the world shows that hopes and aspirations raised by them often remain unfulfilled and cause disappointment in the minds of the people. Often they produce a paradoxical affect: most of them remain too weak to protect the society from human rights violations but at the same time they create an unprecedented demand for such protection. The same is the story of the National Human Rights Commission of India.

Chapter 19

Dysfunctional State Human Rights Commissions

The Protection of Human Rights Act, 1993, (PHRA) was a big leap forward for the protection of human rights in the country. It created a high-powered National Human Rights Commission (NHRC) and made provisions for setting up of State Human Rights Commissions (SHRCs). Initially, for a variety of reasons there was reluctance of the State Governments to set-up SHRCs. But the NHRC strongly favoured creation of such commissions to spread the message of human rights all-over the country and ensure that victims of human rights violations in different parts of the country get justice.

There is no specific mention in the PHRA for the setting up of human rights commissions at the level of Union Territories. As early as in 1994, the NHRC in its Annual Report strongly recommended that the Government of India should set-up Human Rights Commissions in Union Territories as well to facilitate decentralized grievance redressal.

At present, Human Rights Commissions are functioning in twenty one states. But at the initial stages, many of the states were dragging their feet. One of the reasons behind reluctance of the State Governments to set-up State Commissions has been the resource crunch. Many North-Eastern State Governments were also of the view that incidents of human rights violations in their states were few and would not justify the creation of a SHRC with a Chairman, who has to be the present or former Chief Justice of a High Court and three other members. Delhi State Government had earlier expressed unwillingness to set-up a State Commission on the ground that that the NHRC was already carrying out the function that would be performed by the State Commission and it might not be obligatory in legal terms to set-up a State Commission. NHRC, however, strongly advised the Delhi Government to reconsider its decision because Delhi is the third highest among all states in respect of complaints filed before the NHRC. The Delhi Government later on fell in line and set-up a State Commission.

The State Government of Uttar Pradesh issued a notification to establish a State Human Rights Commission in April, 1995. However, in view of the delay in setting up of the Commission, a PIL was filed in the High Court of Allahabad in 1998. During the pendency of the petition, the State Government cancelled the notification under section 21(1) of PHRA to render the PIL infructuous. However, Allahabad High Court took serious exception to this and directed the State Government to set-up a State Human Rights Commission within four months.

Protection of Human Rights Act (PHRA) provides that the SHRCs will consist of a Chairman and four members. Amendment of the Act in 2006, limits it to a Chairman, who has to be a Chief Justice or a former Chief Justice of a High Court and two other members to be appointed amongst persons having knowledge of or practical experience in matters relating to human rights. The reason behind the unwillingness of many State Governments to set-up Human Rights Commissions is not just financial crunch, but an apprehension that findings of such Commissions in different complaint cases will embarrass the government. This precisely happened in West Bengal, when a former Chairman of the Commission, who was a Supreme Court judge pulled up the State Government in many human rights violations cases and much to its annoyance directed it to pay compensation to the victims.

Unfortunately, experience over a stretch of time shows that many of the SHRCs have become dysfunctional and failed to advance the cause of human rights in the country. Disenchanted complainants prefer NHRC to SHRCs to file their complaints. Some of the inadequacies plaguing most of the SHRCs are poor complaints-handling procedures, lack of accessibility to common people, particularly, those belonging to marginalized groups, and dearth of trained and sensitized staff. Websites of most of these Commissions are not functional and do not provide relevant information regarding the status of the pending cases. Again, most of them are in English, making it difficult for the local people to understand them. Record-keeping in most of the SHRCs is poor and most of the SHRCs' staff have no training, experience or orientation in matters concerning human rights.

Very often, the complainants are not informed regarding the progress of their cases. SHRCs operate from the comfort zones of state capitals and have shown little inclination to go down and function at the district level. Human Rights Law Network (HRLN), a civil society group, made a study of the functioning of the SHRCs and came to some unflattering conclusions. It found that some of the SHRCs like that of Kerala and Assam Human Rights Commissions do not bring out annual reports or any significant reports on a regular basis. In Assam, over the years, the Commission has become known for its failure to deliver justice through its orders and judgements. The intelligentsia in Assam views the Commission as a parking lot for retired judges and career politicians. The Andhra Pradesh SHRC also suffers from lack of credibility and is being viewed by the academics and activists as an ineffective institution that has failed to protect the human rights of the people.

Many of the SHRCs do not investigate complaints lodged before them by their own investigating staff and solely rely on other agencies of the State Government to carry out the investigation. As most of the complaints are against the police, reliance on the state police for investigation does not inspire confidence. Chairman and members of many of the SHRCs do not command credibility and viewed by the public as pliant occupants who kowtow to the government and seldom take up cudgels even when there is brazen violation of human rights. The unflattering conclusion of HRLN that most of the SHRCs function like another department of the government is not far from truth.

Moreover, jurisdictional controversies between NHRC and SHRCs often have a retarding impact. The Act has not delineated properly their respective jurisdictions. Section 36(1) of the PHRA lays down that the NHRC will not enquire into any matter pending before the State Commission or any other Commission duly constituted by law for the time being in force. Experience shows that this section has been used to thwart the purpose of the Act. This is being done by bringing the matter before the SHRCs in a slightly modified manner to block the jurisdiction of the NHRC. NHRC proposed amendment of the PHRA to vest it with power of judicial superintendence over the SHRCs. But this amendment proposal has not been accepted by the Government. The result is that very often NHRC and the SHRCs fail to act in tandem and at times, work at cross purposes. NHRC's oversight over the SHRCs has become more urgent after amendment of the PHRA, which allows NHRC now to transfer complaints to SHRCs.

Of late, NHRC is extending help to SHRCs in complaints handling processes. It has helped Maharashtra State Human Rights Commission to implement a complaint management system for speedy disposal of the complaints. The NHRC has now also constituted a committee to carefully look into the issues of minimum manpower and financial requirements of SHRCs in order to strengthen and help them to discharge their functions effectively.

Poor functioning of the SHRCs is a matter of serious concern. In a vast country like India, well-equipped and functional SHRCs can provide decentralized grievance redressal mechanisms and immensely help the cause of human rights protection by working in close collaboration with NHRC. SHRCs have belied the expectations of the people and failed to play that role. Further, many a State Governments are now treating SHRCs in a most cavalier manner and turning a deaf ear to their recommendations. The decline and degeneration of the SHRCs adversely impact the cause of human rights protection in the country. Paradoxically, most of them are too weak and ineffective to protect society from human rights violations, but at the same time, they have created an unprecedented demand for such protection.

Chapter 20

National Human Rights Commission: Is it a Toothless Tiger?

The Chairman of National Human Rights Commission (NHRC) has rued that the Commission is a toothless tiger. It is unequal to the task of combating effectively human rights violations because it lacks power to issue legally enforceable orders. Its recommendations may or may not be accepted and implemented by the Government. The NHRC is a high-powered Commission presided over by a former Chief Justice of the Supreme Court. Its members include a judge of the Supreme Court, one from the State High Court and two other members with knowledge of and experience in matters relating to human rights. However, under the Protection of the Human Rights Act, 1993 (PHRA), it can only make recommendations and not issue orders penalizing persons or authorities responsible for violation of human rights and awarding compensatory relief to the victims. It has to depend upon state or Central Governments for giving effect to its recommendations. This can at times be irksome as well as frustrating.

This statutory constraint has handcuffed the Commission since its inception. The Commission has now and again railed against the limitations and constraints on its functioning imposed by PHRA and strongly pressed for amendments of various provisions of the Act that have shackled it. At the instance of the Commission, a high-powered committee chaired by Justice A.M. Ahmadi, a former

Chief Justice of Supreme Court, delved deep into the matter and gave a cogent report for amendments of the various inhibiting provisions of the PHRA. Unfortunately, the recommendations of the Commission for the amendment of the Act based on the report on the Ahmadi Committee were stonewalled for a long time by successive Central Governments. The amendments of the Act, which came after an interval of more than a decade (Amendment of the Protection of Human Rights Act 2006), only made some tepid and insignificant amendments and ignored most of the key recommendations of the Commission. Hence, there is very little likelihood of the government developing sadden concern for the protection of human rights and providing the Commission with "teeth to bite".

But a careful and objective appraisal of the ground realities shows that the situation is not so gloomy and hopeless. I had worked as the first Director General (Investigation) of the Commission. Those were the halcyon days of the Commission. It commanded prestige and authority and most of its recommendations over various issues starting from deaths in police and jail custody, starvation deaths in different parts of the country, bonded labour etc. were accepted by the Government. Indeed, more than 90 per cent of the recommendations were accepted and very few were turned down or put in cold storage. I understand even now, by and large, recommendations of the Commission receive due attention and consideration and not peremptorily turned down.

Normally, Human Rights Commissions and Institutions set-up in different countries of the world on the basis of Paris Principles, 1991, only make recommendations. They do not try to usurp the role of courts by issuing binding orders. The role of Courts and Commissions are complementary and not antagonistic. National Human Rights Commissions or Institutions are not judicial bodies and do not purport to make enforceable decisions. They generally make recommendations and proceed less formally than the courts. The quasi-judicial authority is structured less to provide particular substantive relief, but more to provide a forum that is distinct from the judicial process. This extra judicial jurisdiction has proved to be an effective instrument for addressing issues of systemic violation of human rights. It may be mentioned that some NHRIs have been able to establish their reputation and credibility and the courts have increasingly relied upon them in dealing with problems relating to violations of human rights. In India, the Supreme Court has often sought the help of the NHRC in enquiring into the cases of human right abuses and sending reports to the court for further follow-up action.

There is also another side of the coin. Decisions of the Commission remain open to judicial reviews. Hence, against the orders of NHRC, if they become enforceable there will be appeals to the courts. This may create a tricky situation that may tie up the NHRC in protracted judicial process and hinder its effective functioning. NHRC officers will have to frequently run to different courts with consequent loss of time and energy. At present NHRC receives a large number of complaints from various parts of the country (almost 90,000 complaints a year) which bespeaks of the yearning of the people for trouble-free expeditious justice.

Again, from a wider perspective it can be said that binding orders are often grudgingly and reluctantly obeyed but cogent and well argued recommendations can bring about systemic changes and improvements. Quite a few recommendations of NHRC on custodial justice, prison reforms, child marriage, bonded labour, starvation deaths have been accepted by the government and helped the cause of advancement of human rights.

Shirley Heafy, a former Chairperson of Royal Canadian Mounted Police Public Complaint Commission (RCMP) has very aptly observed that "*a truly remedial institution may not be best served by 'teeth'. An order grudgingly accepted and implemented can change only one result. A recommendation if it is persuasive and compelling can change a mindset*".

Though the Commission can only recommend and not bring to book the malefactors in cases of violation of human rights, it has awarded interim relief (compensation) to the victims in a large number of cases. The original Act empowered the Commission to recommend relief to the complainant on completion of enquiry. In 2006 Amendment, Section 18(c), now enables the Commission to recommend relief at any stage of the enquiry. Further, the Commission can approach the Supreme Court or the High Court for such directions or orders or writs as that court may deem necessary if its recommendations are cast aside. In case of violation of human rights by private persons, the Commission can intervene by looking into the failure of police, or public authorities to prevent violation of human rights.

There is no doubt that the NHRC acts under serious statutory constraints. The Government is also not willing to make it a vibrant and effective watchdog of human rights by making important amendments of the Act like enabling the Commission to enquire into violation of the human rights by the armed forces, conferring financial and administrative autonomy to the Commission, enlarging the definition of the human rights embodied in Section 2(b) of the Act and giving it an overseeing role over the State Human Rights Commissions. But within these limitations and constraints, the Commission can play and has played an effective role as a human rights watchdog. It showed great courage and commitment by taking *suo moto* cognizance of the communal holocaust in Gujarat and indicted the State Government for its failure to control it. It also brought to the centre stage social, economic and environmental rights of the people and their relevance in the universe of human rights. Instead of bemoaning, NHRC has to play a more proactive and transformative role for the advancement of human rights in the country.

CHAPTER 21
Cross Border Trafficking in Women from Nepal

Devastating earthquakes in Nepal have caused unprecedented loss of lives and properties. The massive calamity has devastated Nepal and caused untold human misery and sufferings. Unfortunately, the disastrous natural calamity has also provided an opportunity to the traffickers to carry out their nefarious operations of *"trade in human misery"*. It is reported that human sharks are on the prowl. They are taking advantage of the situation seeking to traffick young girls from Nepal. Many of these girls, who have lost touch with their families are desperately seeking shelter. They are being lured by the traffickers with the promise of shelter and jobs.

Cross-border of trafficking of women for commercial sexual exploitation from Nepal to India is continuing unabated for a long time. The action-research study on *"Trafficking in Women and Children"* sponsored by the National Human Rights Commission and conducted by the Institute of Social Sciences estimated that about 5000 to 6000 girls are trafficked from Nepal to India every year. Trafficked Nepalese young girls are in demand because of their fair complexion and because of the prevailing myth that sleeping with virgins can cure sexually-transmitted diseases. Traffickers take advantage of the poor economic condition of many Nepalese families and lure their girls by promise of jobs or marriage. Nepalese families, who are in dire economic straits become easy victims of the traffickers.

It has been found that in Nepal, traffickers have nexus with politicians, officials, police, customs, transport agencies, etc. Besides, using false promises of well-paid employment, false love, marriage, traffickers play the role of 'guardians' for girls and women, often in the guise of helping them to seek medical treatment, or helping them to reach their relatives in India. In South-east Nepal, women of Badi caste were traditionally entertainers, who offered cultural shows as well as sexual services to local kings, religious leaders and landlords. Trafficker gangs capitalized on this local tradition and incorporated Badi community into a cross-border sex trafficking ring. Furthermore, women who are divorced, or victims of rape, face enormous level of social stigma and ostracized by their families. This makes them vulnerable to trafficking.

The Indo-Nepal border is a long porous border with specific entry points along the entire stretch. This facilitates extensive illegal cross-border movements. Under 1950 Treaty with India, there is no immigration control of the Nepalese travelling or migrating to India and so no records are maintained. Though Nepalese women are trafficked to many Indian cities, Mumbai happens to get the highest percentage of them. The booklet "*Rape for Profit*" brought out by Human Rights Watch, 'Asia' describes how girls are picked with promises of job or marriage, etc., by pimps and traffickers.

Durgadas Khemeri, a well-known social worker of Nepal, who has rescued many Nepalese girls from brothels of Mumbai, describes how many of the victims were duped by their professional husbands, who after marriage sold them to the brothel owners. Out of them, nearly 60 per cent contact HIV/AIDS. Kept in virtual slavery, they are unable to negotiate any aspect of the situation. Unfortunately, no meaningful steps have been taken either by the Government of India or the Government of Nepal to firmly tackle the situation. While there has been some acknowledgement by Government officials in both the countries about the magnitude of the problem and the need for action, neither India nor Nepal has taken serious measures to stop trafficking. "*Despite a plethora of national and international instruments that addressed trafficking and abuses common in industry, the trade continues to prosper*" (*Rape for Profit*. – Human Rights Watch/Asia, p. 5).

It is a hard fact that both India and Nepal have not displayed any earnestness in combating trans-border trafficking. In India, Suppression of Immoral Traffic Act, 1986, to combat trafficking has proved to be inadequate. The Act makes prostitution the only form of trafficking and does not include other forms of trafficking as enunciated Palermo Protocol. The Immoral Traffic Prevention Amendment Bill, 2006, which broadens the definition of trafficking, by including all forms of enslavements from servitude to prostitution and shifts the blame from victim to the perpetrator, has not yet been enacted to law.

Various studies conducted on implementation of Immoral Traffic Prevention Act in India show that provisions of the Act deal with traffickers and exploiters are seldom invoked, whereas Section 8 of ITPA wherein the victims can be charged and prosecuted for soliciting are over-used.

Jurisdictional limitations also contribute to hinder effective trans-national anti-traffic operations. Today, trafficking has become a vast international operation. Tentacles of the traffickers are spread over different countries and combined international action is called for to deal with the growing menace. Traffickers and exploiters have no boundaries but law-enforcement officers are bound by limitations of jurisdiction. There is need for a national data base and a national task force, duly empowered to take up investigation of such crimes.

The SARC Convention envisages setting up of a task force for dealing with trans-border trafficking. Since the Convention has been ratified by all the member countries, the task force should be set-up, without any delay. To start with, informal networks including NGOs, should be institutionalized so that they can carry out jointly anti-trafficking operations with greater vigour. Some *ad hoc* committees set-up at the initiative of local law enforcement agencies on U.P. - Nepal border are doing some useful work. It is a pity that while there exists a close nexus between traffickers and pimps on both sides of the border, meaningful cooperation between the law enforcement agencies of both the countries is missing. Earlier, in a regional meeting of senior law enforcement officers of both Nepal and India (22nd October, 2000) to combat cross-border trafficking, a body of professionals called South Asia Professionals against Human Trafficking (SAPAHT) was constituted to fight trafficking in women and children and enhance cross-border collaboration and information exchange. Unfortunately, it did not get off the ground.

In this connection, it may be mentioned that to combat trafficking in persons, the American Congress has passed an Act known as Trafficking Victims Protection Act, 2000. The Act lays down that "*USA will not provide non-humanitarian, non-trade related foreign assistance to any Government that does not comply with minimum standards for elimination of trafficking, and making significant effort to comply with such standards*". Both Nepal and India have been placed in Tier II Watch List for not firmly complying with 'Trafficking Victims' Protection Act' (TVPA) minimum standards.

Index